THE AUSTRIAN EXAMPLE

The Austrian Example

KURT WALDHEIM

Translated by Ewald Osers

The Macmillan Company

New York, New York

To Cissy

The Macmillan Company
866 Third Avenue, New York, N.Y. 10022
Collier-Macmillan Canada Ltd., Toronto, Ontario

The Austrian Example was originally
published under the title *Der
Österreichische Weg* by Verlag
Fritz Molden, Vienna.

Library of Congress Catalog Card Number: 72-94012

Printed in Great Britain

Contents

FOREWORD

The present book does not pretend to be an exhaustive history of
Austrian foreign policy before and after the Second World War.
It merely highlights the salient developments, the emphasis being
placed on the period after 1945 when the author participated in
the formulation of Austria's foreign policy and in the implementation of some of its essential phases. The presentation of events
of the interwar period aims at facilitating the understanding of
developments after the rebirth of the republic.

My main purpose in writing this book was to stress the special
position of Austria in the interplay of forces on the world scene
and to bring out the role that a neutral country like Austria can
play in world affairs. Political thinking and public attention concentrate nowadays mainly on the role and action of big powers
endowed with vast territories, large populations and tremendous
scientific and economic capacity, not to mention armaments. The
rest of the world is all too often seen in terms of zones of influence, alliances or as a poverty-stricken 'Third World'. Little
attention, if any, is being paid to neutral countries and to their
contribution to world peace and order. In this book Austria's
attempts to make such a contribution through a policy of 'active
neutrality' are given as an example.

I also wanted to underline the close relationship between
domestic policy and foreign policy. A stable foreign policy is
nowadays unthinkable without a healthy internal policy, and vice
versa. In our increasingly interdependent world, internal and external policies of nations are moving closer together. Science and
technology, the spread of the industrial revolution and of the
peoples' aspirations for peace, progress and justice throughout

the world, are narrowing the distance between internal and external interests, national and world interests, internal and foreign affairs. Mankind is beginning to realize that in the absence of world government, world peace, justice and order are essentially the result of peace, justice and order maintained within nations and among nations. The same applies to the management of our planet's resources and environment. This book gives an example of the interplay of external and internal forces with regard to a small but strategically placed country. To grasp these relationships and to draw from them the necessary conclusions is one of the first duties of today's political leaders.

The co-operation of all political forces in Austria after the Second World War has allowed the country, against the greatest odds and difficulties, to regain its freedom and independence. By pursuing this course Austria did and does render a great service not only to her own security but to the development of a peaceful Europe and to world *détente* in general. The unity of a people round a foreign policy aimed at peace, co-operation, non-intervention in other countries' domestic affairs, friendship with all other nations and active participation in the world's collective organizations can give it a very useful role to play in world affairs. For several decades Austria as such was absent from the world scene. The adoption of a policy of permanent neutrality and of active international co-operation has brought her back as an honoured and useful partner in world affairs.

This book was originally published in Austria in 1971. The present edition has been brought up-to-date, and opening and concluding chapters have been added.

I wish to extend my sincere thanks to colleagues and friends who gave me their advice and help in the preparation of this book.

INTRODUCTION

In 1918 the Austro-Hungarian Empire, one of the greatest political entities of Europe for several centuries, collapsed. It ranked as the second largest European country in size and the third largest in population. Like many European countries, it was the outgrowth of a long and complex history of territorial acquisitions and losses through conflicts and marriages.

While other European powers were looking overseas and were engaged in colonial policies, the Austro-Hungarian Empire was beset with internal problems due to the national aspirations of its various ethnic groups. To the north of it, since the time of Bismarck, a new pole of political power had emerged with vast ambitions in Europe and overseas. The industrial revolution had placed Europe in the forefront of world affairs. Big national powers were grafted on old monarchies or on young republics born from new political and social aspirations. Outside Europe the industrial revolution's only significant gain was North America, where a combination of favourable conditions was giving it its greatest upsurge.

The Austro-Hungarian Empire paid the price for its involvement in the origins of the First World War. The monarchy disappeared. Several ethnic groups took their freedom. A handful of democratic leaders of the new Austrian Republic fought for the survival of a country reduced overnight to a fraction of its former size and population, and beset with the most tragic economic hardships. Their attempts to break from isolation through plans for a Danube confederation or an economic union with Germany were doomed from the outset.

Versailles and Saint-Germain designed the new political patterns of Europe, based on ethnic aspirations, alliances, the dismemberment of the enemy and on strategic and economic interests. The stage was set for one of the most complex periods of bilateral diplomacy and alliances the world had ever seen. At the same time a first attempt at international solidarity and co-operation was made via the League of Nations. But the United States, after its decisive intervention in the war, withdrew from the European scene. The United States Congress did not support President Woodrow Wilson's attempt to create the beginning of a world order and so the League remained a purely European affair, an adjunct to bilateral diplomacy, a covenant largely of European nations.

For the Austrian leaders this period meant a long struggle for political assertion and for the economic survival of the small alpine republic in the web of European diplomacy.

The absence both of a stable balance of military power in Europe and of an international order created a political situation that was bound to give birth to adventurism. Hitler saw his opportunity and managed to mobilize forces for the most ruthless series of conquests, making a mockery of international law and totally disregarding even the most elementary human rights. Nationalism, exacerbated by claims of racial superiority, was given its most extreme and abhorrent form. Diplomacy and all other rules of accepted international conduct collapsed in front of this show of crude force. Austria did not have the slightest chance in such a gigantic game. The attempts by the Austrian leaders to lean on Italy were of short duration. Austria became the target of the whole gamut of ideological and political subversion and terror of which the Nazi regime was capable. But this was only the prelude to the *Götterdämmerung*. On 12 March 1938 German troops marched into Austria. The republic disappeared from the map of independent countries. Of the empire at the beginning of the century there remained nothing. A country had reached the lowest point of its history.

The Second World War was a real world war encompassing countries from all continents: Japan, a country which as recently as 1905 had remained outside the mainstream of the industrial revolution; the United States, this time fully involved in the conflict; the Commonwealth countries of Africa, Asia and the Far East which supported the United Kingdom; the French colonies which gathered round General de Gaulle; and many other less developed countries which provided resources for the war effort and entered into the modern world.

As the war was nearing its end the Allied powers in Teheran and Yalta set out to plan and design the new Europe and world which was to emerge from the holocaust. Dismemberment of the enemy, military occupation, restoration of vanished countries, modifications of borders and the establishment of a better world order were the main subjects of the Allied consultations. Austria was re-established as a country but subject to four-power occupation.

Regarding world order, an immense step forward was accomplished by creating the United Nations which, through a membership reaching from the USSR to the United States, Latin America, Asia and the Far East, became the world's first truly international political organization.

World relations soon turned sour again: the wartime alliance collapsed, the cold war set in, the globe was divided into two armed camps. During that period Austrian leaders were bent on one sole objective: to achieve Austria's independence and freedom from occupation. The means chosen to accomplish this objective were: to avoid joining any pact or military alliance; to establish Austria as a permanently neutral country under conditions acceptable to all great powers; and to mobilize internal public support for those aims.

This policy succeeded and led to one of the most remarkable, if not unique, postwar settlements in which the big powers and a small country, situated in one of the most sensitive parts of the world, were involved.

One of the main external factors that led to this result was the policy of peaceful coexistence initiated by Nikita Khrushchev. The Russian premier wanted to demonstrate to the world, by means of a concrete example, that he was serious in his policy. The western powers had already given their agreement to a draft treaty that was the result of many years of negotiations between the big powers and Austria. The main internal causes of the success were the determination of the Austrian leaders, the support of the Austrian people and the patient negotiations that took place with the former Allied powers.

The result was also of benefit to the rest of the world: a country located in a highly sensitive area, right on the lines of contact of big power zones, established itself on the basis of its permanent neutrality as a centre of stability. This contributed significantly to a lessening of tension in Europe and to an improvement of relations between the big powers. It is true that the settlement of the Austrian problem was facilitated by a factor that is not found in other divided countries: the new republic was endowed from the start with a unitary government and was not divided into separate governmental entities or administrations, each supported by different ideologies or external powers.

The treaty ending Austria's occupation that was signed on 15 May 1955 at the Belvedere Palace in Vienna by the foreign ministers Vyacheslav Molotov, Harold Macmillan, John Foster Dulles, Antoine Pinay and Leopold Figl opened a new chapter in the history of the Austrian republic. In December of the same year a further aspiration of the Austrian people was fulfilled: Austria became a member of the United Nations. As a permanently neutral and independent country she was expected to play a role again in the community of nations. Her leaders and people wanted her to play a useful and dynamic role based on the special position occupied by Austria between the big powers and on the principle of active neutrality, i.e. neutrality in the inter-play of alliances but commitment to international policies and actions that are beneficial to the community of nations, reduce tensions, consolidate peace and further economic progress and justice throughout the world.

Several ways were suddenly open to Austria for an active foreign policy on the world scene: participation in efforts designed to knit Europe more closely together, to reduce divisions and tensions in that area and to consolidate Europe as a peaceful and stable continent; participation in the development effort of the poorer parts of the world through bilateral and multilateral aid, thus helping to reduce North–South tensions; and, above all, active participation in the world-wide efforts of the United Nations and of its specialized agencies concerned with the international aspects of virtually every human endeavour on earth.

In other words, when Austria recovered her sovereignty in 1955 and committed herself to permanent neutrality she entered a different world: a world of many independent nations on all continents; of various economic and social systems; of all degrees of economic development; a world consisting of big atomic powers and of small and medium powers; a world of great cultural diversity; a world of heavily and sparsely populated areas growing at different rates; a world kept in peace by an equilibrium of atomic terror but also by the efforts of a global organization; a world already rendered interdependent by science and technology but still deeply divided politically.

A new trend was also emerging to mark the history of postwar political relations; the height of the cold war was over and a slow but steady process towards peaceful coexistence and cautious *détente* had begun among the big powers.

The history of Austria's foreign policy since 1955 has been a history of active involvement into this new world context. She decided to play a full and active role in the international community and lent her services to any efforts at *détente*, for any progress on these two fronts would mean consolidation of her own security and survival. Vienna became the seat of two important UN agencies, the International Atomic Energy Agency and the United Nations Industrial Development Organization, thus making her, with Geneva, another European centre of the United Nations. The Austrian capital became host to many international conferences, among which was the first UN conference ever held on outer space. Austria also played an active part in UN peacekeeping operations. The Salt Talks between the USA and the USSR, one of the most crucial efforts to achieve disarmament in postwar history, are conducted alternately in Helsinki and Vienna. Whenever she can Austria today plays an active role in every organ, specialized agency and humanitarian programme of the United Nations, in the deep conviction that the maintenance of peace, security and progress in the world at large is an indispensable means to preserving her own independence, peace and prosperity. Through suffering, isolation and annihilation Austria has learned that in our modern interdependent world to be an active partner in the world community is not only a privilege but a very serious responsibility. Austrian leaders are convinced that in order to reap benefits from world co-operation a nation must also contribute its best to that co-operation.

One of the essential objectives after the signing of the peace treaty was to take Austria out of her isolation and to anchor her again in international reality. As a precondition it was necessary to define clearly her position. A country of the size of Austria has two possibilities: it can join an alliance or it can adopt neutrality. Today, seventeen years after the decision of the National Assembly on Austria's permanent neutrality, we can say with satisfaction that this decision was the right one. It gave the country unprecedented political stability as well as great economic prosperity.

The conversion of the Austrian people to such a policy was not an easy matter. Neutrality was a totally new concept to the Austrians, who for centuries had been taking an active stand in virtually every European conflict. However, neutrality binds the state, not the individual citizen, and does not involve ideological neutrality. Austria, for example, is certainly not ideologically neutral and definitely practises democracy in the western sense. When judging Austria's neutral policy, we must also remember that the people had to undergo, within a few short years, a change of basic thinking that in other neutral countries took several decades if not centuries.

Thanks to internal political peace and to external stability Austria was able to create for herself abroad, after the signing of the treaty, an image that is quite remarkable when compared with the size and the population of the country.

Calculated restraint coupled with initiatives taken at the right moment have allowed Austria to become a positive factor in international politics. There can be little doubt that the existence of a neutral Austria is indispensable to the equilibrium between East and West. The conclusion of the 1955 treaty must in the last resort be ascribed to that fact. While giving back to Austria her sovereignty it also placed very special responsibilities on her shoulders. The geopolitical position of Austria within the contact zone or testing-ground of the great ideological power-groups of our time has given this small country a meaning that is far from that of a *quantité négligeable*. The well-known saying of the Czech historian Palacký that 'if there were no Austria, one would have to invent it' applies no less to the small Austria of today than it did to the monarchy. Even the great powers recognize this. But their support of Austria's neutrality will last only as long as it is in their interest. It is therefore the duty of Austria to create confidence through her policy of neutrality and to avoid any action that would undermine such trust.

This might seem simple to many people but in reality it is not. Quite the contrary: such a policy is much more difficult than that of a country bound by an alliance. The latter can, at any moment, consult its ally and on most vital issues will follow the same policy. In return it is assured protection in case of danger. The situation is totally different in the case of a neutral country: it must rely entirely on itself; it must reach its own decisions independently on the basis of a thorough analysis of all aspects of a given situation. Any error in judgement or any emotional involvement may lead to wrong decisions that can have disastrous consequences for its neutrality.

Herein lies the danger but also the great challenge to Austria's foreign policy. The neutral state can rarely escape from taking its responsibilities. On the contrary, it must take a clear stand on most international issues in order to prevent suspicion and doubt.

From time to time, Austria's foreign policy is accused of lacking glamour. We cannot reject such a criticism strongly enough. It would indeed be a grave mistake for a neutral country to try to attract world attention through dramatic declarations or actions. It might mean a temporary appearance of the country's name in the headlines of world news, but the political consequences would be disastrous. Many such declarations by well-known politicians have in the past aroused much publicity and created a host of misunderstandings that contributed to international unrest. The foreign offices of the countries concerned then had the difficult task of repairing the damage by correcting, redressing or explaining the statement that had been made. A foreign policy of sensationalism is contrary to the interests of a neutral country. Reason, cool-headedness and continuity are infinitely more necessary than dramatization.

A journalist who complained to one of our postwar statesmen

that one seldom heard anything about Austria in the world press received the answer: 'The less written about us the better it is, for it means that there is peace and order in our country.' Good diplomacy does not seek the limelight. It finds its reward in the fact that a country is successfully pursuing its way.

Neither simplification nor complication are helpful in foreign policy. But simple common sense is not sufficient either: exact knowledge of the facts and circumstances, a realistic appraisal of the forces at work and a good grasp of historical interconnections are required. The international play of forces leaves no room for sentiment. A foreign policy can be successful only if it pays heed to these requirements.

The Ballhausplatz in Vienna had a decisive influence on world affairs for several centuries. Today Austria's diplomats represent a small state. International policy, thanks to rapid scientific and technical change and its effects on the power position of states, is determined to a large degree by the bipolar or tri-polar development of the two or three super-powers. But the 'little ones' have not lost their significance. Since they are deprived of any real power, there is all the more reason for them to demonstrate their usefulness to other nations through an intelligent, well thought-out and often conciliatory foreign policy, thereby also serving their own interests.

In 1971 the UN General Assembly voted that the People's Republic of China should take its rightful seat in the world organization and in all its organs. An important step forward was thus accomplished towards the universality of the world organization. One of the most populous countries on earth joined other countries in the collective effort born from the holocaust of the Second World War to build a better world. The historical significance of that step may still take several years to be fully appreciated.

During the same General Assembly, the appointment of a new secretary-general came up. There were several candidates from the neutral and developing countries. Numerous factors play a role in the appointment of a secretary-general. There is little doubt, however, that two considerations greatly influenced the 1971 election: the position of the candidates and of their countries of origin as neutrals *vis-à-vis* the big powers and their position as men who could understand the aspirations, problems and difficulties of the medium, smaller and poorer nations.

The selection of the Austrian candidate by the Security Council and the General Assembly was certainly based on these fundamental considerations.

Each secretary-general pledges through his oath of office his care and concern exclusively to the objectives of the charter and to the service of the community of member nations. But each secretary-general also remains influenced by his origins and by the experience acquired during his earlier active life. This is only natural and that is why the antecedents of each candidate are scrutinized so carefully by the members of the Security Council.

There can be no doubt that the example of Austria's foreign policy and the part I played in it have left a certain imprint on me. Thus I cannot fail to be realistic and pragmatic, fully aware of the special role and weight of the big powers in present world affairs. But I also know from the Austrian example that such powers can get together to solve a problem, especially if there is a smaller country involved which shows internal unity and determination and which is ready to work actively for a solution. I further believe that under the pressure of today's global problems and with the determined help of the medium and smaller nations a new great alliance can and must be re-established among all powers within the United Nations. The world does not need a new political cataclysm to provoke such an alliance. Poverty, hunger, the lack of proper education, health and shelter, the new problems of the environment and of our endangered seas, waters and atmosphere are big enough problems to justify the co-operation of all forces in the United Nations. The instrument is here, created under the impact of the horrors of the Second World War. It is universal in scope and almost universal in membership. All that is needed is for the leaders of today to use it, support it and meet on the solid basis of its charter.

I further believe that the United Nations and their secretary-general have a crucial role to play in consolidating by all possible means the process of *détente* that has begun. This new trend in postwar political relations constitutes a great opportunity for humanity and for all nations, big and small. There have been many incidents and accidents on that road, but it is reassuring that none of them has so far seriously interrupted the process. The United Nations can play a vital role in forestalling conflicts, in stopping them, in preventing flare-ups from turning into wider conflagrations and in solving existing unsettled issues. Any success of the organization in preventive and curative diplomacy will facilitate the process of *détente* and of better understanding among all states. It should be part of the historic role of the United Nations to provide the machinery and the framework necessary for conflicting powers to relax their tensions and to reach accommodation among themselves and with other nations. This is why I intend to offer the secretary-general's good offices resolutely whenever I am convinced that the United Nations under its charter can and should assist states in solving international problems. Governments may decide not to make use of these offers, but they will realize in the end that the United Nations, despite its limitations, which we must correct, is still the most advanced instrument ever devised by humanity for its collective security. It is reassuring in this respect that most of the conflicts brought before the United Nations and dealt with by the organization are today either solved or in a state of armistice or truce. Of course all too often the patient is brought to the United Nations when it is too late. This situation also obviously needs to be put right.

Another lesson that I have learned from the Austrian example is that no foreign policy can succeed if it is not fully understood and supported by the people. This applies equally well to the international efforts of nations. It is indispensable that public opinion be well informed about the possibilities as well as the limitations of the world's collective efforts through the United Nations and its agencies. After the Second World War exaggerated hopes were placed in the organization. All too often in the minds of the public the United Nations is mistaken for a world government with legislative and executive powers, and is expected to solve directly every problem on earth, from peace and security to economic development, the environment and the drug problem. This is not the case and it must be made clear to the public that the United Nations is based on the co-operation of sovereign member states. On the other hand governments may be vastly more inclined to support and to use the United Nations and to implement its recommendations if there is strong public opinion in favour of the organization. The people themselves therefore have a crucial say in world affairs. Support and realistic appraisal by the public could be the razor's edge between war and peace. In a matter as serious as world peace and the United Nations we must guard equally against unrealistic hopes and destructive cynicism.

Nobody can claim today to know what tomorrow will look like. There will be many adaptations, many changes, much need for reciprocal learning among nations, governments and peoples. Great new problems unknown today will emerge and old beliefs will be shattered or deeply modified. But we all know very clearly what we want: we want peace, progress, justice, the preservation of our planet and respect for the rights of all peoples. Twenty-seven years have now passed without a world war. We are of course still far from a world of peace, order and justice. But with realism, pragmatism and hard work it is not impossible that humanity may at long last enter into a period of lasting peace and understanding. We need such political progress in order to concentrate our efforts on the global problems that will confront our planet in the decades to come. Some of my views in this respect are outlined in the last chapter of this book.

In one of the museums in Vienna a bird's-eye view is given of the fate of a human community situated in a strategic geopolitical situation on the river Danube, at a crossroads of civilizations, on a main route of human migrations between North and South and East and West. Roman soldiers stood at this place, called Vindobona, behind the wall built on the shores of the protecting Danube. A city was born there which grew progressively round its cathedral. Protecting walls surrounded it and were torn down and rebuilt further and further away leaving place for what are today the 'Rings' of Vienna. At one point in history walls were no longer necessary. Vienna became the capital of an empire that lasted for several centuries. That empire disappeared and Vienna remained as the oversized capital of a small country. That country at one point disappeared. The city was heavily bombed and damaged during the Second World War. But the country was reborn and its capital shines again today and has become the centre of ever-increasing international activity. Let us hope that the spirit and the attitude that have made such a development possible will continue to strengthen international relations towards a world at peace without want and fear. May Austria's example be of some value to the community of nations.

BIRTH FROM CHAOS

Only a nation with confidence in itself can survive in the long run. A country's foreign policy can be successful only when it is based on internal political stability and when there can be no doubt of the people's determination to remain independent. In Austria today all these conditions are fulfilled. Things were different between the two wars, when public support for Austria's independence was by no means a matter of course. At that time the curious phenomenon of her readiness for surrender was due to two causes. The first of these was the severe psychological shock of the collapse of the Austro-Hungarian monarchy and the imposed peace of Saint-Germain, which saddled a truncated Austria with responsibility for the First World War. Europe's second largest state in area (after Russia) and the third largest in population (after Russia and Germany) was suddenly transformed into the Austrian Republic, with 32,000 square miles and about $6\frac{1}{2}$ million inhabitants. Moreover the economy of this truncated country had been tailored to the vast extent of the old monarchy and was therefore in no position to meet the needs of the new political unit.

Famine and suffering attended the cradle of the First Republic. From this public despair sprang the wish to associate with the larger political unit of the German Reich, with which the Austrians felt themselves linked by language and culture. Then, after an interlude of economic recovery, came the Depression, when the disastrous crash of the New York Stock Exchange on 29 October 1929, triggered off a mass collapse of the banks of Europe. As the army of the unemployed increased, the political climate in Austria deteriorated and a conviction that this new Austria was not viable on her own began to gain ground.

The history of Austria's foreign policy reflects the domestic and economic development of the country, since its every move was, as it were, predetermined because no alternative existed. This situation began in 1919, when successive Austrian governments had to take their foreign policy decisions with an eye to averting a disastrous famine and were ready to make any concessions in return for the promise of food supplies. This situation was repeated when at the very last moment the government had to avert national bankruptcy brought about by inflation, and again a few years later when it had to avoid the total collapse of the country's economy after the bank crash.

In the autumn of 1918, as the war was drawing towards its close, the Emperor Karl I had tried to ensure the survival of the Habsburg Empire by transforming the monarchy into a federation.[1] This was not a new plan. Work on it had been going on for many years, but its realization had always been prevented on the one hand by the irreconcilable conflict between German nationalists and Slavs, especially the Czechs, and on the other by Hungary's refusal to grant autonomy to the nationalities in its half of the empire. By October 1918 it was too late. The Hungarians invoked the emperor's manifesto to dissolve their union with the Austrian half of the empire. In the event this did not help them much: if anything, Hungary was treated by the victorious powers even more harshly than Austria. Meanwhile the other nationalities took advantage of the creation of national parliaments, decreed by the emperor, to declare their independence or to unite with sister nations beyond the old frontiers.

Thus in Prague Czechs and Slovaks proclaimed themselves an independent republic (Czechoslovakia); Croats and Slovenes united with the Serbs to found what became the kingdom of Yugoslavia; the Italian territories in the south of Austria united with Italy; Galicia became part of the republic of Poland; and Bukovina and Transylvania became parts of the kingdom of Rumania. An internal political measure, taken for foreign policy reasons – to achieve a more favourable basis for peace negotiations – thus had far-reaching consequences on foreign policy: in fact it involved the complete redrawing of the political map of the Danube region.

On 21 October 1918 the German-speaking deputies of the old imperial parliament had met in Vienna to set up a provisional national assembly in line with the imperial manifesto. The regions they represented were basically those of modern Austria, but with the addition of the representatives of the South Tyrol, southern Styria and above all Germans from Bohemia – from the Czechoslovak border regions subsequently to be known as the Sudetenland. There were also German-speaking population groups scattered throughout the territory of the monarchy, for instance in Bukovina, Transylvania and southern Hungary. In terms of political alignment the deputies represented three main trends – the Christian Socialists (70 deputies), the Social Democrats (39 deputies) and the German Nationalists (101 deputies). Only the Social Democrats declared that they were republicans. The only ones to be regarded as 'loyal to the empire', and then only up to a point, were the Christian Socialists. The German Nationalists had always accused the House of Habsburg of favouring the Slavs; they now proposed that Austria should be incorporated into the German Reich.

The proclamation of the Czechoslovak Republic on 28 October and its immediate recognition by the Allies meant the collapse of all hopes of preserving at least a large federation of the nationalities within the monarchy. The position of the Provisional National Assembly had thus become questionable, since a fair number of the deputies represented constituencies that were now part of the territory of the new Czechoslovak state. Preservation of the monarchy in Austria was of no interest to those territories. The only hope of resisting the Czech claims seemed to lie in immediate incorporation into the German Reich.

There was the additional hope that a clear dissociation from her monarchist past might ensure that Austria would be given better treatment by the victorious Allies. The provisional national assembly therefore decided to proclaim a republic – not only from domestic considerations but largely on foreign policy grounds. This step was made possible by the Emperor Karl's abdication from the functions of government.

WHAT REMAINS IS AUSTRIA

When the new Republic was established on 12 November 1918

and adopted the name 'Deutschösterreich' ('German Austria')
the deputies of the Provisional National Assembly proclaimed
its annexation to the German Reich almost unanimously. But the
young state was beset by the most serious problems concerning
foreign policy from the very hour of its birth. Austria's politicians
were slow to free themselves from the concepts of the old
monarchy and of the federal ideas expressed in the October
manifesto, and their persistent claims to speak on behalf of the
Germans within the frontiers of Hungary, Czechoslovakia,
Poland, Rumania, Yugoslavia and Italy were bound to lead to
conflicts with these neighbours and former compatriots. The
interplay of domestic and foreign policy was emerging clearly, as
it was to emerge again in subsequent years.

Admittedly, after the first proper elections for the Constituent
National Assembly on 16 February 1919 the German Nationalist group in Parliament shrank to 26 deputies, who were opposed
by 72 Social Democrats, 69 Christian Socialists and three
deputies of minority parties. But even this parliament had been
elected on the basis of an electoral law of December 1918 which
had not merely defined the state's territory as present-day
Austria but had also laid claim to the German-speaking areas of
Czechoslovakia, the South Tyrol, southern Carinthia and southern Styria. It goes without saying that in the Sudetenland the
Czechs prevented the population from participating in these
elections and that in southern Carinthia or southern Styria there
could be no question of elections at all, since the Yugoslavs had
marched into these territories, just as the Italians had marched
into the South Tyrol, declaring them, in anticipation of the peace
treaty, to be integral parts of their country. Of Austria's immediate neighbours Czechoslovakia, Yugoslavia and Italy belonged to
the victorious powers. It was with these three countries that the
sharpest conflicts had existed from the outset, because nearly four
million German-speaking former Austrians had come under the
rule of these countries as a result of the defeat of Austria.

Political ideas at the time were governed largely by the concept of a nation's right to self-determination, as proclaimed by
President Wilson of the United States in his famous 'fourteen
points'. In fact this principle was applied only to the victors and
was denied to the conquered in the First World War. In the case
of Austria this was true of the South Tyrol, southern Styria and

the border regions of Bohemia and Moravia. Only in two instances was the principle applied – in southern Carinthia, where Italy did not wish to see Yugoslavia, her new rival on the Adriatic, gain yet more power, and in western Hungary, in present-day Burgenland. The peace treaties of Saint-Germain and Trianon stipulated that a plebiscite was to be held in southern Carinthia, whereas Burgenland was to be ceded to Austria at once. The plebiscite in Carinthia was a clear victory for Austria. In Burgenland a compromise solution was adopted and a plebiscite was held in the regions round the town of Ödenburg (Sopron in Hungarian), the majority voting for Hungary. The Allied intention behind this measure had been the creation of a permanent conflict of interests between Austria and Hungary. This conflict was so acute that disputes over the occupation of Burgenland even resulted in clashes between Austrian and Hungarian army units. Austria and Hungary had certainly been prevented from moving closer together and perhaps recreating a miniature edition of the former Danube monarchy. Even though Hungary had possibly been mutilated even more terribly than Austria by the Trianon Treaty, fifteen years were to elapse before any common policy was embarked upon once again.

In Vienna meanwhile the Provisional National Assembly had entrusted the government of the country to a state council consisting of twenty members and presided over by the state chancellor, the Social Democrat Dr Karl Renner. The state secretary for foreign affairs was Viktor Adler, the recognized leader of the Social Democratic Party, but he died on the evening of 11 November, before the proclamation of the republic. His successor was Dr Otto Bauer, who was to remain the leading intellect in Austria's Social Democratic Party for the next two decades, and also of its radical wing, which was known as Austro-Marxism. Bauer's aim was to gain Italy's support for the rejection of Yugoslavia's claim to the southern regions of Carinthia and Styria and for Allied permission for Austria to join the German Reich. The condition, of course, was a restoration of the traditional friendship between Berlin and Rome, which had existed since the war of 1866 but had been interrupted by the First World War. Bauer was evidently expecting that Italy would now acknowledge German endeavours of 1914 and 1915 which at the time were aimed at convincing Austria to make concessions to Italy. The obstacle to such a policy was of course the South Tyrol. Bauer worked out a plan under which the entire Tyrol was to be proclaimed neutral, to such an extent that in the event of war it would be occupied by the Swiss army.[2] But Italy had not the slightest intention of giving up the South Tyrol and saw no reason to promote Austria's annexation to Germany. Her main objective was to thwart any attempt at establishing a Danubian federation. This was in line with her policy of smashing the Danubian monarchy, which proved successful in spite of hesitant support from France and virtually no support at all from Britain.

A strange feature of this development, in terms of foreign policy, is the fact that in Vienna at that time only two alternatives seemed conceivable – the formation of a federation in the Danubian area or Austria's incorporation into Germany. Any other solution, it was thought at the time, would leave Austria unable to survive. In fact the Allies decided in favour of this third alternative. In this way they prevented the German Reich from getting too powerful and also prevented the emergence of a new power centre in the Danube region, but the settlement left central and south-eastern Europe dangerously divided and weakened both politically and economically. It was a political line that met the wishes of chauvinist politicians in Prague, Bucharest and Belgrade, and probably also reflected the attitude of the majority of the people in the successor states, but it was certainly not a far-sighted policy. The seeds sown then were to be harvested in the years after 1938.

The question of Austria's annexation to Germany was right at the top of Dr Otto Bauer's list of foreign policy problems. Ideological reasons certainly played a considerable part in this. He believed in a Marxist Greater Germany and – not unlike his German Nationalist opponents – saw the *Anschluss* as the only hope of solving the question of the German minorities. Also, he was a much more inveterate opponent of the monarchy than, for instance, Karl Renner. His activity was therefore oriented towards achieving an *Anschluss* and preventing the establishment of a Danubian federation, which seemed to him to entail the danger of a Habsburg restoration. Bauer's intentions were viewed in Berlin with considerable reserve, but a secret agreement defining the conditions for Austria's annexation to Germany was signed on 2 March 1919. This agreement was of course destined to remain a worthless scrap of paper, since the decision had been made without the consent of the Allies.

The four years or so that had elapsed since the outbreak of war had led to a total disorientation concerning the views and intentions of the Allied governments. Vienna knew virtually nothing of what was in store for Austria. The warnings of Austrian diplomats, for instance from Switzerland, were assessed as over-pessimistic since neither the government nor indeed any Austrian politician were prepared to believe that the Allies were really and truly seeking to smash Austria. Yet the Allies really had decided on a hard line, as typified in the dictum of Edvard Beneš (later to become President of the Czechoslovak Republic): 'Destroy Austria-Hungary!'[3] As a result various diplomatic initiatives remained largely fruitless, including the mission of the last imperial premier, Heinrich Lammasch, to Switzerland, where he had to make contact with Allied diplomats and emissaries.

Meanwhile in Vienna an Allied high commission had arrived to see that the stipulations of the Armistice were observed. Conditions were chaotic, as they were in the provinces. The population was hardest hit by the breakdown of food supplies. Famine was rife in the towns, infant mortality increased alarmingly, the first symptoms of inflation appeared. In an atmosphere of appalling depression, political confusion and misery, annexation to the German Reich seemed to offer the only glimmer of hope. That was why the slogan of the *Anschluss* was received with cheers and applause at numerous public demonstrations. In some of the provinces unofficial plebiscites were organized in which the overwhelming majority supported association with Germany. The only exception was Vorarlberg, where 80 per cent of the population demanded annexation with Switzerland.

Austria's international contacts were virtually confined to Switzerland and the neutral Scandinavian states. In this situation it is not surprising that the Social Democrat Otto Bauer, as secretary of state for foreign affairs, should have viewed the reports of former imperial diplomats with a certain measure of distrust, with the result that the members of the Allied high commission in Vienna were Austria's only direct link with the western world. In March 1919 the Austrian government, virtually for the first time, learned what it had to expect. The peace treaty with Germany, the British Colonel Cuninghame disclosed, would be exceedingly harsh. Austria could hope to receive slightly better treatment only if she voluntarily renounced the idea of an *Anschluss*. Even so her excessive expectations must be radically reduced. Any part of the German-speaking areas of Moravia and Bohemia, the South Tyrol and the German-speaking part of western Hungary could be retained by Austria, or be assigned to her, only if she dissociated herself unequivocally from the German Reich. A short while later the French ambassador, Allizé, declared that the Allies would suspend the dispatching of foodstuffs to Austria unless *Anschluss* propaganda was stopped immediately. But it soon became increasingly clear that Italy was not prepared to give up the South Tyrol and the Allies were not inclined to apply the principle of self-determination to the Germans in Czechoslovakia.

To make matters worse, Austria now found herself threatened along her eastern frontier as well: in March 1919 the Communist Béla Kun had come to power in Budapest and proclaimed a Government of Councils. There was heavy fighting between Czech and Hungarian troops in Slovakia and later between Rumania and Hungary, ending eventually in Béla Kun's defeat and escape. But until then there was very real anxiety about the possible penetration of Hungarian Red Army units into Austria and indeed of a Communist rising in Vienna itself, where units of the *Volkswehr* – the new Republic's armed forces, raised from remnants of the old army – were openly displaying sympathy for the radical left wing.

But the heaviest blow to Austria came with the attack by Yugoslav troops, who launched two thrusts in late April and May in an attempt to seize Carinthia. News was also coming in from Prague and Belgrade about intensive propaganda there in favour of liquidating Austria in such a way that eastern Austria would be shared between the Czechs and the Yugoslavs. Thus a Slav corridor was to separate what was left of Austria from Hungary, with the border running immediately outside the gates of Vienna.

The Vienna government had to remain passive in the face of all these developments. The only action open to it was to dispatch *Volkswehr* units to Carinthia to support the local troops and home-guard formations in their defensive fighting. Even this was possible only because Italy was anxious to prevent her neighbour Yugoslavia from acquiring any further territory. But Dr Bauer had hardly any ways of championing his policy before the world, though he did try to gain support for Austria's cause among his political friends in France and Britain and, as already mentioned, hoped to be able to play a part in the great interplay of forces by leaning towards Italy on the one hand and promoting Austria's *Anschluss* to Germany on the other.

The Allies' strict prohibition of an *Anschluss* soon made it clear that the German card could not be played and indeed that any emphasis on co-operation with Berlin would be detrimental to Austria's interests. Moreover on 28 June 1919 Germany signed the Peace Treaty of Versailles, Article 80 of which concerned the recognition of Austria's independence. Italy, for her part, felt that her main aim must be to prevent the Germans from reaching the Brenner Pass and to stop Yugoslavia growing too powerful. Thus Otto Bauer had to acknowledge that his policy had foundered. But even his resignation, submitted on 26 July 1919 and intended to meet Allied objections to him and to facilitate the Austrian delegation's negotiations at Saint-Germain, proved pointless. His successor, Dr Karl Renner, who was simultaneously state chancellor, state secretary for foreign affairs and leader of the Austrian delegation to the peace negotiations of Saint-Germain, was unable to alter the harsh conditions imposed by the Allies.

THE PEACE THAT WAS NO PEACE

The Paris peace conference had opened at the Quai d'Orsay on 18 January. The invitation to send a delegation to Saint-Germain-en-Laye arrived in Vienna on 2 May[4] and ten days later the Austrians, led by Dr Renner, set off. But in Paris there was no chance of negotiations whatever. The delegates were first taken to the Château of Reinach and later to Saint-Germain itself, where they were treated like prisoners and excluded from all contact

with the public and with the other delegations. On 2 June they were eventually taken to a session of the conference. They were presented with the peace treaty, a document of more than three hundred pages, which, in the words of Georges Clemenceau, the French premier, did not even contain all the stipulations. The Austrians were to study the text and submit 'new observations or documents' within a fortnight. Dr Renner pointed out that a truncated Austria could not be saddled with the legal inheritance of the Danubian monarchy: surely all successor states to the Habsburg Empire were jointly responsible? But no one apart from the Austrians would accept this view at Saint-Germain.

The draft treaty surpassed the Austrians' worst expectations. The German-speaking areas of Bohemia and Moravia, and even parts of northern lower Austria, had been assigned to Czechoslovakia, while the South Tyrol had been handed over to Italy and southern Styria to Yugoslavia. Only the question of Carinthia was still open.

This meant that all the preparatory work done in Vienna for the negotiations had now been superseded. The directives given to the delegation by the National Assembly proved to be illusions – the right of self-determination, or at least autonomy, currency union with Austria and military neutralization for the German-speaking areas of Bohemia, Moravia and Austrian Silesia. As for the South Tyrol, there had been hopes that it would be returned to Austria in its entirety, though Austria would have been prepared to make the Tyrol neutral and to offer Italy the right to maintain garrisons in the South Tyrol. It had also been expected, almost as a matter of course, that the German-speaking areas of southern Styria, like the whole of Carinthia, would remain Austrian. And now Austria, to add insult to injury, was to sign an obligation to pay reparations, the extent of which had not even been settled.

Vienna had taken the view that all successor states should jointly take over both the assets and the debts of the Dual Monarchy in appropriate quotas, and that this principle should also be applied in the event of reparations payable to the victorious powers. This was Austria's attitude on the status of the republic under international law. Vienna consistently rejected the Allied theory that a legal continuity existed from the Austrian half of the old monarchy to the Austrian republic – after all, the two halves of the empire had not been regarded as two separate entities under international law before 1914 – and instead held the view that the Dual Monarchy had perished through 'dismemberment' and that Deutschösterreich had emerged by revolution on 12 November 1918, in the same way as had the other states that had been formed from the former territory of the monarchy. Austria had not therefore been in a state of war with any power and had not declared war on anyone, and nor had war been declared on her by anyone. Professor Hans Kelsen, who had drawn up the Austrian constitution, had formulated this idea as early as December 1918 but the Allies rejected this legal concept because it would have jeopardized their reparation claims against Austria.

The idea of Austrian neutrality emerged in connection with the discussion of the peace terms. Proposals ranged from making separate parts of the state territory neutral to the neutrality of the entire state. But these ideas remained ineffectual at the time because the Allies were pursuing the foundation of a League of Nations as a peace concept. Such an organization was based on the idea of collective security, which would lay the foundations for a new order in Europe and throughout the world. Collective security, as understood at that time, excluded neutrality.

The Austrian peace delegation was made up of politicians, diplomats, experts and representatives of those areas that had declared themselves for Austria. Without any doubt it included excellent experts, but they had hardly a chance of using their skills to Austria's advantage. Even the carefully prepared documents were scarcely used, as the Austrian delegation had not been invited to the negotiations since its arrival in Paris. There was thus no possibility of contacts or information. The delegates were not even informed about the progress of the negotiations and their only communication with the peace conference was in writing. It is doubtful whether their 'submissions' were ever examined. The only ray of light during these many weeks of waiting was an appeal by the Allies to the Yugoslav government to suspend all military operations in Carinthia and to respect the armistice line.

The second version of the peace treaty, handed over on 20 July, assigned to Austria modern Burgenland, a region of western Hungary with about 250,000 inhabitants. But the county of Pressburg (now Bratislava) was given to Czechoslovakia as a last remnant of the plan for a Slav corridor to the Adriatic.

Under these conditions the ban on the *Anschluss*, stipulated in the peace treaties of Versailles and Saint-Germain, seemed to deprive Austria of her last hope for the future. A fact which her delegates overlooked was that, in the interests of balance of power in Europe, the Allies could not really have acted otherwise since union with Austria would have made Germany, in spite of having lost the war, stronger than the empire of 1914.

Article 88 of the Treaty of Saint-Germain stipulated:

The independence of Austria is inalienable otherwise than with the consent of the Council of the League of Nations. Consequently, Austria undertakes in the absence of the consent of the said Council to abstain from any act which might directly or indirectly or by any means whatever compromise her independence, particularly so until her admission to membership of the League of Nations, by participation in the affairs of another power.

Thus there was reluctance to spell out a downright prohibition of annexation to Germany,[5] though there could be no doubt about the practical significance of this formulation. It was merely in the interests of the balance of power in Europe that Austria should not join any state, whether Germany, Italy or any other state. The Paris peace conference set up Austria as an independent political structure within her existing frontiers. At the same time Austria was assured that she would be admitted to the League of Nations. She joined the League in December 1920, at roughly the same time as such states as Switzerland, Finland, Sweden, Norway and Denmark; Germany, on the other hand, was not admitted until 1926.

The treaty imposed on Austria against her will in 1919 had made no provision of any kind to ensure that, following the destruction of the vast economic sphere of the old monarchy, the new state would have an economic foundation that would enable it to survive. Here lay the seeds of future crises.

The provisions of the peace treaty were accepted by the National Assembly on 10 September 1919. In accordance with the stipulations of the treaty the name of the state was changed to 'the Republic of Austria'.

The first task facing those responsible for Austria's foreign policy was to overcome her neighbours' mistrust and fear of a Habsburg restoration. This was made more difficult by long-standing hostility and Austria's desperate supply situation made her an ideal subject for political blackmail attempts. If they were threatened with the suspension of food or fuel supplies the Austrian government quite simply had no answer to give in negotiations with foreign countries. Only the disinterested aid schemes implemented by Switzerland, the Netherlands, the Scandinavian countries and others saved the urban population of Vienna from starvation. The country's economy, already bled white by more than four years of war, was strained to breaking-point by the harsh stipulations of the peace treaty. The destruction of the extensive economic sphere of the old monarchy, which had resulted not only from the last war but also from a lack of foresight on the part of the Allies, deprived Austria of virtually all hope. Amid the hardships of the postwar period she was quite simply unable to readjust to her new situation as a small country. The great majority of heavy industries, as well as a substantial part of the production of consumer goods, had been in what was now Czechoslovakia, as had the raw materials such as coal that were so desperately needed by what was left of Austria. Oil had come from Galicia, foodstuffs from the agricultural surplus regions of Hungary and from Croatia. Alternative sources for all these supplies now had to be found as a matter of urgency, since the frontiers with the newly created states were almost insuperable obstacles. Austria was clearly unable to surmount them on her own. On top of the general shortage of industrial products, raw materials and food supplies there was now the added problem of inflation, since the currency of the old monarchy, the crown, was valid only on the territory of the Republic of Austria. Old banknotes, which had at first been valid in the successor states, were flooding back into Vienna, while new currencies were being introduced in Prague, in Budapest, in Zagreb – throughout the successor states. Totally impoverished, Austria saw setting the banknote printing presses in motion as the only means to salvation. All these factors produced financial instability that ended in headlong inflation. The only salvation would have been for other countries to grant her credits. But these were either too slow in coming or too small. There was famine in the country, the un-

B

employed took to the streets and hunger demonstrations became the order of the day. A permanent internal political crisis soon developed which the government did not succeed in overcoming, though it made desperate efforts to do so.

AUSTRIA'S STRUGGLE FOR EXISTENCE

On 11 June 1920 the coalition government of Social Democrats and Christian Socialists broke up. It was succeeded by a 'proportional cabinet' made up of members of both parties, which continued, after a fashion, to work together.

The conservative forces in the country, above all the Christian Socialists, were gradually recovering from the shock of the collapse of the monarchy. They began to realize that they still commanded considerable support among the population. In the short term, thanks to the Social Democrats' powers of organization, the workers were in a position to control the situation, but in the long run they were too weak to hold power. Communist-type Republics of Councils had collapsed in Hungary and in Bavaria. Throughout Central Europe there was a perceptible swing to the right. The world revolution was not going to take place. It was at this point that an alarming phenomenon first appeared, one that would hardly seem imaginable today – the emergence of defence associations and armed party formations.[1]

Heimwehr formations had been formed in various provinces as early as 1919. In Styria and Carinthia they had been organized as frontier guards and had played an important part in repelling Yugoslav attacks. In Upper Austria, Salzburg and the Tyrol these formations emerged as a reaction to the Bavarian Communist dictatorship that had recently been overthrown. In the industrial regions on the other hand, workers' militias came into being, similarly equipped – sometimes with Allied approval – from imperial army stocks. From them grew the *Republikanischer Schutzbund*, the army of the Social-Democrat Party.

The main problems facing the new government were how to put an end to famine, the drafting of the constitution and the *de facto* acquisition of Burgenland. In spite of many difficulties the proportional cabinet succeeded in enacting the constitution of September 1920 which had been drafted by Professor Hans Kelsen. This represented a compromise between the federalist interests of the provinces and the centralism of Vienna; generally speaking this compromise was more in line with Social Democrat ideas (a two-chamber system, a federal council with a delaying veto, a federal president with limited authority).

On 17 October 1920 new elections were held. They brought bitter disappointment to the Social Democrats, for the Christian Socialists, with 79 deputies, emerged as the strongest party. The Social Democrat seats dropped to 62, while the Greater German Party won 18 seats and there was one Independent.

Michael Mayr now formed a Christian Socialist cabinet, while Michael Hainisch was elected federal president. On 21 June 1921 the Chief of Police in Vienna, Dr Johann Schober, became chancellor. Inflation was by then assuming alarming proportions.

On 4 June 1920 Hungary had signed the Trianon Treaty, which had assigned Burgenland to Austria, and in December of that year the Allies had called on her to relinquish the region. The situation had been further complicated by two abortive attempts by the Emperor Karl to reassume the throne of Hungary in the spring of 1921. The Allies eventually stipulated that 27 August 1921 should be the date for the *de facto* handing-over. Under Hungarian and Italian pressure Austria eventually agreed to hold a plebiscite over Ödenburg, which resulted in the town being lost to Austria. But she did take possession of the province of Burgenland.[2]

In the field of foreign policy the dispute with Hungary led to a *rapprochement* with Czechoslovakia. On 16 December 1921 Schober concluded the Lana Agreement with Czechoslovakia, which provided a much-needed Czechoslovak credit of 500 million crowns for coal and sugar deliveries, but at the price of express recognition of the frontiers. This meant a final renunciation of the Sudeten areas. The Greater German Party left the government and in May 1922 overthrew the Schober government while the chancellor was attending a conference held in Genoa to discuss economic matters with the Allies.

On 31 May 1922 Dr Ignaz Seipel, a priest and Christian Socialist politician, formed a new government. The immediate problem was the recovery of Austria's financial situation which, as a result of inflation, had come to seem hopeless. The economic situation was still disastrous. Austria was in the position of a beggar who was barely able to satisfy his most pressing needs by accepting minor loans. The crown had dropped to a fraction of its former value, war bonds had become worthless and the middle classes were impoverished. Seipel tried first of all to stabilize the currency by means of internal loans. His plan, in which a considerable part was played by Dr Viktor Kienbock, the finance minister of the day, and by the banker Dr Kunwald, envisaged halting the printing of paper money and laying the foundations of a healthy currency by establishing an independent issuing bank. But the Länderbank and the Anglobank, which were predominantly French and British owned, withdrew their initial promise of support and thus all hopes were once more dashed. An appeal for help by the federal president to the West remained unanswered. It was pointed out to the Allies that without aid the government would no longer be able to run the state.

But the use of threats of self-annihilation was not Seipel's method. It remained his aim to convince Austria's neighbours and the signatories to the treaty of Saint-Germain of her peaceful intentions and to explain to them that her survival was vital for peace in Europe. By means of a series of negotiations in Czechoslovakia, Germany and Italy – a masterpiece of diplomacy – Seipel succeeded in realizing his aims within a few weeks. He next turned to the League of Nations and, in the favourable atmosphere engendered by this world organization, achieved his first aim. On 4 October 1922 he signed the 'Geneva protocols', which provided for a joint British-French-Italian-Czechoslovak loan to Austria to the tune of 650 million gold crowns. The creditors included the principal signatories to Saint-Germain, who thus demonstrated their interest in Austria's economic recovery. Austria, for her part in accordance with Article 88 of the treaty, undertook not to give up her independence for twenty years.

These foreign policy declarations show that this agreement was not merely of economic importance but had far-reaching political effects. Austria was adopting a very definite international standpoint which, though not expressly defined as neutrality, came close to such a position by its political content.

In 1932 Austria was to receive a second League of Nations loan from Britain, France, Italy and Belgium on the same terms.

But economic recovery required first and foremost the application of a severe austerity programme which involved making a hundred thousand civil servants redundant, a currency exchange at a rate of 1:10,000 and the introduction of a turnover tax. The recovery programme represented a vital step along the road to economic reconstruction, though it entailed considerable sacrifice – at first the number of unemployed rose.

With the League loan Seipel had at last laid the real foundation-stone of a new Austria. For the first time there was a return of confidence in the viability of the country, no matter what her future would be. Seipel's tragedy was that his work was only partly successful. After the League loan he did not want to enter into any further foreign policy commitments. In 1923 he visited Budapest, Belgrade, Rome and Warsaw in order to clear up some unresolved political issues and to stabilize Austria's relations with her neighbours. The numerous arbitration agreements that Austria signed during the next few years (with Hungary, Poland and Italy, for example) reflected her wish to maintain good relations with all states.

Opposition from within his own party led to Seipel's downfall in November 1924. Dr Ramek, a Christian Socialist from Salzburg, now formed a cabinet, with Dr Mataja as foreign minister. Mataja tried to return to closer collaboration with the successor states of the Danube region but he encountered rebuffs on all sides. Towards the end of 1925 relations with Rome had become so tense over the policy of Italianization in the South Tyrol that there was even talk of a military conflict, while misunderstandings on foreign policy issues further confused the situation. In 1926 Seipel formed a new cabinet which united all the middle-class parties. The foreign policy outlook gradually improved and Austria began to look forward to a calmer period. The Locarno Pact, by which Germany established a security system with Belgium, France, Britain and Italy, and Germany's entry into the League of Nations resulted in a further *détente*.

In Paris in 1926 Seipel had impressively championed the idea of international understanding. Relations between the former

Allies and Germany should, in his view, be improved pragmatically. Count Coudenhove-Kalergi's Pan-European Movement, which was born in Vienna, was busy mapping out new roads which should enable a European solution to be found for the Austrian problem as well. But although the mid-twenties had witnessed a marked improvement in several sectors of Austria's economic life – in line with an economic upsurge throughout Europe – there had been no real restructuring of the economy to meet the needs of a small country.

The parliamentary elections of 24 April 1927 brought the Christian Socialists heavy losses. Seipel did manage to form another government, but the Opposition felt that the tide was flowing in its favour and parliamentary work made slow progress. Finally the 'Schattendorf trial', in which a jury acquitted a group of organized ex-servicemen who had fired at members of the *Schutzbund*, resulted in a concatenation of unfortunate circumstances which culminated on 15 July 1927 in demonstrations in Vienna. These soon turned into a full-scale rebellion. The Social Democrat leadership lost control of the inflamed mob – the Ministry of Justice was set on fire, police stations were stormed, barricades were erected and the fire brigade was prevented from putting out the blaze. Eventually the police, who had suffered a number of casualties themselves, opened fire. A large number of dead and wounded made up the bloody balance-sheet of the day. Irreparable damage had been done by a chain of mistaken reactions on the part of the Social Democrat leadership and the police. In spite of a general strike the Seipel government remained in office. The Opposition labelled Schober a 'workers' assassin' and Seipel a 'prelate without mercy'. In 1929 Seipel eventually resigned.

Summing up Seipel's foreign policy, we can say that it was based on the fundamental principle of avoiding systems of alliances, of not entering into close relations with other countries or risking serious disputes – certainly no easy task in view of Austria's geopolitical situation. He vigorously supported an active League of Nations policy and believed that one day a European solution of the *Anschluss* problem would emerge of its own accord. It was these considerations that made him favour the Pan-European Movement.

The domestic difficulties with which Austria's democratic and parliamentary form of government was faced were aggravated by anti-parliamentarian trends abroad. These included the rise of Fascism in Italy, Hitler's attempted *putsch* in Germany in 1923 and Josef Pilsudski's dictatorial form of government in Poland in 1926, as well as that of King Alexander of Yugoslavia in 1929. Meanwhile Hungary was being ruled in a patriarchal and ultra-conservative manner by Admiral Horthy, the Regent. These developments could not fail to have an effect in Austria. The events associated with the burning of the Ministry of Justice were an indication of the new radical mood that had sprung up in the country. Further clear evidence of this was the development, since July 1927, of the *Heimwehr* movement and the *Schutzbund*.

Although the trend towards political radicalism was discernible in Central Europe by 1928, the international situation was nevertheless marked by a seemingly unbroken economic upsurge and by the success of the policy of international *détente* and collective security. Admittedly these successes were of a psychological rather than a practical nature (as with the Briand-Kellogg Pact).

As we have seen, 29 October 1929 went down in the history of the United States and of the world as a day of disasters. Stock exchange prices on Wall Street crashed to bottomless depths; banks and industries collapsed. Economic depressions in the United States had had detrimental effects on Europe before – but the New York crash of 1929 and its consequences outdid anything known in the past. Even Britain, the classic country of free trade, went over to protectionism in the form of 'imperial preference', i.e. the preferential treatment of members of the Empire. Nearly all economically important countries in the world withdrew into a kind of economic nationalism and tried to find a substitute for dwindling world trade on their home markets. Austria, as a small country, could not follow this road with any degree of success. Besides, the few years of reconstruction had not been enough to restore her economy or to give it a completely new structure. Thus she became one of the first countries to feel the worldwide economic depression to its full extent.

In the United States the political radicalism that followed in the wake of worldwide destitution was checked by President Roosevelt's 'New Deal'; in Germany, on the other hand, the immediate result was the rise of National Socialism. Its effects on Austria were unmistakable. Governments followed one another in rapid succession. In March 1931, Johann Schober, now foreign minister, tried to achieve a customs union with Germany through secret negotiations. But when the German foreign minister, Dr Curtius, arrived in Vienna a strong protest was immediately lodged by France, the Little *Entente* and Italy, who saw the customs union merely as an attempt at a 'hidden *Anschluss*'.

At the end of May 1931 the Creditanstalt in Vienna, the last big bank dating back to the monarchy, collapsed. The whole of Central Europe was now in the grip of the depression, a situation that in Austria promoted the rise of National Socialism, which until then had carried no weight whatever.

RADICALIZATION IN CENTRAL EUROPE

The storm clouds were rapidly gathering over Europe. The main event of 1932 was the 'Tardieu Plan', which was intended to provide for closer economic co-operation among the Danube states and to replace for Austria the rejected Schober–Curtius customs union. But the Tardieu Plan was wrecked by German and Italian opposition. Once more Austria received no help and economic hardship grew worse. Political radicalization was inevitable in these circumstances.

On 20 May 1932 Engelbert Dollfuss, until then minister of agriculture, became federal chancellor. No one believed that his government could survive for long, and the urgently needed second League of Nations loan received parliamentary approval with only the narrowest of majorities. On 4 March 1933 the three presidents of the National Assembly* resigned for relatively trivial reasons bound up with parliamentary tactics and thus enabled Dollfuss to prevent the Assembly being recalled. Without realizing at first what it had done, Austria's parliament had thus eliminated itself. Dolfuss ruled by decree on the basis of the controversial wartime economy special powers act of 1917.

In Germany meanwhile National Socialism had seized power. In Austria the significance of this event was fully realized – which is more than can be said of some countries of Western Europe

* The *Nationalrat*, the lower chamber of the Austrian parliament.

whose attention was focused primarily on their economic difficulties.[3]

The National Socialist regime in Germany soon began to launch violent attacks against Austria. The 'one-thousand-mark limit' imposed by Berlin paralysed German tourist traffic to Austria, the intention being to deal a fatal blow to Austria's tourism and her entire economy. Although the missing German tourists were offset to some extent by tourists from the rest of Western Europe, this hostile measure still meant a further obstacle to the improvement of the economic situation. Following a number of serious incidents the National Socialist Party was banned in Austria. The result was a violent propaganda campaign from Germany and acts of terrorism in Austria.

The situation indicated the need for co-operation between the Dollfuss government and the Social Democrats, but this was prevented by Mussolini, who demanded a tough domestic line towards the left-wing parties as the price for the international support by Italy that Austria so urgently needed. On 13 April 1933 Mussolini demanded of Dollfuss the abolition of the parliamentary system, the dissolution of the Social-Democrat Party and the formation of a united front on the model of the Fascist Party, backed by the *Heimwehr*. Eventually, on 12 February 1934, bloody clashes broke out between the government and the Social Democrats; such clashes had been only narrowly avoided for several years.[4] The fighting resulted in the deaths of more than two hundred people. Otto Bauer and Julius Deutsch managed to flee the country.

Now the Social Democrats, too, were forced into illegality. As a reward, as it were, the 'Rome Protocols' were signed on 17 March 1934; these envisaged close co-operation between Italy, Austria and Hungary and consisted chiefly of economic agreements. Mussolini's influence on Austria had now been further strengthened. The Austrian public did not welcome this policy for a variety of reasons in which rejection of Fascism and its political methods, the South Tyrol issue and wartime resentments all played a part.

It should, however, be pointed out that Dollfuss was one of the few men to stand up to Hitler, whereas most European politicians tried to come to terms with him. Thus a Polish-German treaty of friendship and non-aggression was signed on

26 January 1934, since the Polish foreign minister, Josef Beck, hoped that it might divert Hitler's aggressiveness towards other targets.

STRUGGLE FOR INDEPENDENCE

On 14 June 1934 Hitler had his first meeting with Mussolini in Venice. The *Duce* was then at the highest point of his career as a dictator and made it clear beyond any doubt that Italy would protect Austria's independence. In order to demonstrate this policy he immediately afterwards invited Dollfuss to visit him at Riccione, where he was on holiday. Dollfuss subsequently had talks with the French foreign minister, Louis Barthou. It seemed as though Austria might possibly gain the support of France, as well as protection from Italy, but it is likely that the contacts made by Dollfuss merely accelerated the National Socialist conspiracy against her independence.

On 30 June 1934, in an operation of unparalleled brutality, Hitler liquidated a number of his opponents in Germany, and in particular the SA chief of staff Ernst Röhm and General Kurt Schleicher, together with several SA leaders and prominent Catholics. He next prepared to strike at Austria.

On 25 July 1934 a group of National Socialist conspirators, disguised as soldiers in the Austrian army, broke into the Chancellery. Dollfuss was gunned down and died of his wounds, without medical assistance or a priest to attend him. A simultaneous coup against the radio building had only short-lived success since the government had been warned – though belatedly – and most of the ministers had managed to save themselves. Soon the radio building had been recaptured and the Ballhausplatz was sealed off. An attempt on the life of the federal president in Carinthia failed. Similar actions were staged by the National Socialists in the provinces, but they all failed. Many of the putschists fled to Yugoslavia. Rome reacted instantly and on the same day several Italian motorized divisions were concentrated in the Brenner area. In view of Mussolini's threat of military intervention Hitler avoided any further actions and the SS and SA units specially organized in Germany for operation in Austria had to remain inactive. National Socialism in Austria had certainly suffered a serious reverse.

At first Hitler tried to achieve a degree of *détente*, sending the former chancellor Franz von Papen to Vienna as his special envoy; since 30 January 1933 von Papen had been his vice-chancellor and because of his flexible attitude towards the National Socialist regime he had managed to stay in office. On 25 July 1934 von Papen took over as head of the German legation. His reception at the hands of the Austrian Federal Chancellery was demonstratively cool. Vienna had no illusions.

Dr Kurt Schuschnigg, who was appointed to succeed Dollfuss on 29 July, intended to continue his policy. On 21 August he had a meeting in Florence with Mussolini, who assured him of his support in the future. Until then Schuschnigg had not been kept fully informed on certain arrangements made between Mussolini and Dollfuss, such as the extent of the measures envisaging Italian military intervention in the event of domestic unrest in Austria. Schuschnigg now told Mussolini that such intervention would be intolerable for reasons of domestic politics. It was soon seen that relations between Mussolini and Schuschnigg would always remain cool, whereas the *Duce* had been on terms of personal friendship with Dollfuss.

In September Schuschnigg met the French foreign minister, a meeting originally planned by Dollfuss. But apart from a French warning against restoring the Habsburgs this produced no concrete results for Austria.

Their ties with Rome put the Vienna government under an obligation. At the beginning of October 1935 Italy ordered her troops to invade Abyssinia, whereupon the League of Nations voted sanctions against her. Austria vehemently opposed this resolution, which had the support of more than fifty member states. Vienna's attitude gave rise to much displeasure, especially in Western Europe.

The most dangerous consequence of this international event for Austria was the fact that the disapproving attitude of the western powers over the Abyssinian issue resulted in an improvement of German-Italian relations. Although Mussolini deeply distrusted Hitler, a gradual *rapprochement* nevertheless developed, if only because Italy was now dependent on German supplies in view of the sanctions imposed against her.

The Laval-Mussolini agreement of January 1935 was also to prove of fateful importance to Austria, though this was not realized in the country at the time. By it all outstanding issues between France and Italy were settled in the style of an *entente cordiale*, but at the price of Italy being allowed a free hand in Abyssinia – though this was not known at the time. The success of the Stresa conference (which opened on 11 April) initially seemed to prove Laval right, since Britain, France and Italy agreed on a common front against Hitler.

The reintroduction of general conscription in Germany (law of 16 March 1935) had preceded the formation of this 'Stresa front'. The Franco-British-Italian treaty was directed against unilateral termination of agreements and reaffirmed support for the Locarno Pact. A Franco-Soviet treaty was signed on 2 May and a Soviet-Czechoslovak treaty on 16 May in Prague – both similarly directed against German rearmament.

Almost as a by-product, the Stresa conference resulted in a reiteration of the Franco-British-Italian declarations of 17 February and 27 September 1934 about the need to maintain Austria's independence and integrity.[5] It was clear that Austria was becoming directly involved in the diplomatic struggle between Britain and Germany about the side that Italy would take. The marked strengthening of the international position of Hitler's Germany in 1936 and the weakened diplomatic position of the western democracies, combined with the strictly neutral attitude of the United States, were bound to have very unfavourable consequences for Austria.

One indication of Germany's diplomatic strength was the proclamation of Belgium's neutrality on 6 March 1936, which meant that the Franco-Belgian treaty of 1920, which envisaged contacts between the two countries' chiefs of general staff and which was directed against Germany, was no longer in force.

By the spring of 1936 Mussolini was anxious to achieve an understanding between Austria and Germany. In order to pacify Hitler he advised Schuschnigg to drop his vice-chancellor Ernst Starhemberg, whose *Heimwehr* he had until then supported in every way. This was no easy task for Schuschnigg in view of the powerful position held by the *Heimwehr*, but it was eventually achieved without difficulty. Thus a stubborn opponent of any collaboration with Germany had been eliminated. This personal success could have given the federal chancellor an opportunity to resume the dialogue with the Social Democrats and to seek a common platform in the struggle against National Socialism. But he failed to do so, and when eventually, alarmed by the growing influence of National Socialism in Austria, he did try to follow this course it was too late.

A COUNTRY IS WIPED OFF THE MAP

In July 1935 the German envoy Franz von Papen had presented the Austrian foreign minister, Egon Berger-Waldenegg, with the draft of an agreement designed to bring about a reconciliation between Germany and Austria. The realization of such a plan had become feasible only since Starhemberg's exclusion from the government. Schuschnigg took the risk of signing an agreement with Hitler, hoping that an express recognition of Austria's independence by the German Reich might prevent her being incorporated into Germany. In retrospect this July agreement in fact represented a decisive step towards Hitler's seizure of power in Austria. Mussolini, who had been asked for 'advice' by Schuschnigg, had long realized that he could not in the long run protect Austria against the massive pressure from her northern neighbour. It therefore seemed to him that to champion an agreement between Vienna and Berlin would be a skilful move in his own policy of checks and balances.

On 9 June 1936 Galeazzo Ciano, Mussolini's son-in-law, became Italian foreign minister. Vittorio Alfieri, a resolute champion of *rapprochement* with Germany, took over at the Propaganda Ministry. Then 11 July saw the signing of the treaty that was to seal Austria's doom. The foreign minister, Berger-Waldenegg, a *Heimwehr* man, had resigned some time before and Schuschnigg had personally taken charge of the ministry. On 11 July he appointed Dr Guido Schmidt as state secretary. In October 1936 the *Heimwehr* formations were dissolved.

The treaty of 11 July 1936 marked a major diplomatic victory by Germany. True, it recognized Austria's full sovereignty – surely a matter of course – and abolished the 'one thousand-mark limit'; Austria in return undertook to acknowledge the 'fact' that she was a German state. This meant that a large number of detained Austrian National Socialists were granted amnesty and a number of German newspapers were admitted into Austria, even though they represented pure propaganda material. Austrian publications, on the other hand, had to take account of the 'fact', which ruled out any frank portrayal of conditions in Germany. The Austrian Foreign Ministry had to see to the censorship of publications directed against National Socialism. Criticism of National Socialist excesses, paradoxical as it may seem, could be disseminated by the Austrian authorities only under the guise of illegal pamphlets.

In view of the signs of weakness shown by the western powers *vis-à-vis* Hitler, the French treaties with the East European states were gradually losing weight. In August 1936 Rumania switched to a pro-German course, and Yugoslavia followed suit in 1937, simultaneously concluding a non-aggression treaty with Italy.

On 20 October 1936 Ciano called on the German foreign minister von Neurath in Berlin. On 24 October 1936 he called on Hitler at Berchtesgaden and Hitler disclosed that he would be ready for war in 1939. On 1 November Mussolini made his first reference to a Rome-Berlin 'axis', in a speech in the Cathedral Square of Milan, though for the time being this remained only a vague term for a policy of collaboration between Germany and Italy.

At the end of 1936 Austria's diplomatic relations with Italy and Germany were deceptively good. From 8 to 12 November the foreign ministers of Italy, Hungary and Austria had talks in Vienna and signed a secret protocol envisaging the adoption of benevolent neutrality by the three countries in the event of war. But the decisive steps were taken elsewhere: on 25 November the anti-Comintern pact was signed in Berlin by Japan and Germany.

In 1937 Austria had a state visit from von Neurath (22 and 23 February), whose proposals for a currency union amounted to Austria's economic annexation to Germany. But Schuschnigg was determined to resist and therefore he sought support in Budapest, Rome and even Prague. On 22 April he had a last meeting with Mussolini in Venice and conveyed his fears to Count Ciano. Mussolini assured the Austrian chancellor of his continued support, firmly rejecting any plans for a Habsburg restoration. And indeed it seems that when Göring visited Mussolini in Rome he did not bring back to Berlin any satisfactory answer on the Austrian issue.

The apparent calm in Central Europe was deceptive. On 5 November a secret conference was held which subsequently received a degree of notoriety thanks to the 'Hossbach Protocol'. It was attended by Göring, von Neurath, General von Fritsch, the war minister, General von Blomberg, Admiral Raeder and Colonel Hossbach as ADC. At this conference Hitler explained his plans for the annexation of Austria and the Sudetenland, which ruled out neither the use of force nor the risk of war. The Austrian general staff thereupon worked out contingency plans for a military defence in the event of a German attack, Lieutenant-General Jansa being the driving force behind this.

On 6 November Italy joined the anti-Comintern pact. After the signing ceremony Ribbentrop also brought up the question of Austria, in a conversation with Mussolini. It is at this point that a decisive shift in Italy's attitude to Austria can be detected for the first time. In reply to Ribbentrop's observation that within the framework of the 'grand policy' made between Rome and Berlin Austria was of only secondary importance, and that this obstacle to joint co-operation should be overcome at a suitable opportunity, Mussolini replied that Austria was not an Italo-German problem but an international one, indicating thereby that his interest in Austria had declined. Thus at long last Mussolini, albeit reluctantly, gave Hitler the green light.

In view of the July agreement the signing of the anti-Comintern pact seemed to rule out the possibility of Austria making any sort of treaty of assistance with Czechoslovakia, possibly under Soviet guarantee. At the last Italo-Austro-Hungarian conference in Budapest in January 1938 an attempt was made to persuade Austria to join the anti-Comintern pact and to leave the League of Nations.

THE NATIONAL-SOCIALIST TERROR

German pressure on Austria was now intensified and the National Socialists in Austria became active once again. When Schuschnigg tried to launch another initiative towards the end of 1937 the right moment had passed. Most of the big names in European politics were no longer ready to receive him. Even earlier, in May 1937, the foreign minister, Guido Schmidt, had been unable to obtain any guarantees for Austria in London or Paris.

France and Britain were seeking a *détente*. On 21 February 1938 Neville Chamberlain appointed Lord Halifax to replace Anthony Eden, who had wanted to adopt a firm attitude with regard to Hitler and Mussolini. Sir Neville Henderson, the British ambassador in Berlin and one of the most extreme supporters of appeasement, regarded Austria's resistance to annexation to Germany as something of a nuisance on the fringe of international events, something that interfered in a petty manner with the grand sweep of political ideas. The French premier, Camille Chautemps, and his minister of finance, Georges Bonnet, also supported the policy of *détente* and had assured von Papen in November 1937 of France's readiness to adopt a conciliatory attitude.

In January 1938 the Austrian police uncovered a National-Socialist plan that provided first for an ultimatum, provoked by organized unrest in Austria, and then for German military intervention. From this moment onwards, if not before, it was clear that the July agreement had failed to achieve its aim.

On 5 February von Papen suggested to Hitler that he should meet Schuschnigg. Hitler agreed and Schuschnigg was persuaded by von Papen that such a conversation might put everything right. Accompanied by Guido Schmidt, he left for Berchtesgaden on 12 February 1938, but when he arrived he was intimidated by a carefully stage-managed reception. He has described his visit in detail. Senior generals, who in fact had no duties at all, were bustling about Hitler's *Berghof*, feigning military activity, so that it looked as if the *Führer* was ready to issue the order for the invasion of Austria at any moment. When he had been subjected to Hitler's usual aggressive and rhetorical tirades and when he had been bowed in and out of a number of rooms at the *Berghof*, with waiting periods carefully spaced out in between, the draft of an agreement was eventually submitted to him. This provided for strong German influence in the Austrian army and for control of the executive by the National-Socialist representative

Arthur Seyss-Inquart. Faced with these massive threats Schuschnigg finally signed.

Back in Vienna the federal chancellor revealed the contents of the agreement piece by piece – but even so it came as a paralysing shock to the people. Apart from a speech on 24 February, in which he publicly outlined his point of view, the chancellor took no action. Not until 9 March, when the government was already in danger of losing control over the executive, did he announce a plebiscite on Austria's future. This was to be held within four days, on 13 March, even though Mussolini had advised against such a step.

Events were now moving at breakneck speed both in Germany and in Austria. Hitler had been taken completely by surprise. Although Schuschnigg was making a number of mistakes in his over-hasty preparations for the plebiscite, he could nevertheless be sure of a majority – a fact that was also obvious to Berlin. Hitler therefore prepared for military intervention. Under extreme German pressure, in the form of an ultimatum threatening invasion by German troops and demanding his resignation, Schuschnigg called off the plebiscite on 11 March 1938 and shortly afterwards resigned. The federal president, Wilhelm Miklas, who refused to entrust Seyss-Inquart with the formation of a new government, yielded to force only when the military attaché of the German legation in Vienna, Lieutenant-General Muff, categorically informed him: 'Unless Field-Marshal Göring has been informed by 19.30 hours that Seyss-Inquart has been made chancellor, 200,000 men now standing by at the frontier will march into Austria. The federal president bears full responsibility for the consequences of his refusal' (quoted from a telephone conversation between Göring and Seyss-Inquart at 17.26 on 11 March 1938).[1]

On 12 March the invasion by German troops began, following an assurance by Mussolini – who had not been informed until the last moment – that Italy would not intervene. On 13 March the 'Reich law on the reunification of Austria with the German Reich' was proclaimed. The parallel Austrian 'Anschluss law' had not been drafted by the Seyss-Inquart government but had been handed over by the Germans ready for proclamation. At this point President Miklas finally refused to put his signature to it and resigned. His office was taken over by Seyss-Inquart, who thereupon signed.

The occupation of Austria represented a breach not only of international law but also of the treaties of Versailles, Saint-Germain and Lausanne, as well as the German-Austrian agreement of 11 July 1936. The official German claim that the Seyss-Inquart government had requested the entry of the German troops – as announced in Berlin on the evening of 11 March – has been proved untrue by historical research. Göring had demanded that such a telegram should be sent so that he would have an alibi for the German invasion to present to the world. In fact not only had Seyss-Inquart not sent the telegram, he had described an invasion as unnecessary, since there were no disturbances.

The question of the ultimate reasons why Austria's independence, which had always been of such vital importance to the European balance of power and to peace, was not upheld cannot be fully answered even today. It essentially boils down to the question of why the great powers failed to stand up in time to the National-Socialist policy of expansion. An important part was clearly played by psychological and, even more, economic factors. One thing is quite clear today – the occupation of Austria by the German Reich was the prelude to the Second World War.

AUSTRIA IN THE THIRD REICH

Austria's occupation by German troops and the end of her sovereignty aroused almost no world reaction. The great powers remained very cool and the few protests that were voiced came from remote countries such as Mexico. Austria's neighbours even expressed their satisfaction and recognized her annexation to the German Reich. A plebiscite held on the *fait accompli* of the annexation on 10 April 1938 was not fully secret and was certainly not in line with democratic procedure. It resulted in a 99 per cent 'Yes', which certainly cannot be regarded as an expression of the popular will. Nor can the plebiscite be considered a justification for the occupation under international law.

The National Socialists celebrated the *Anschluss* enthusiastically. Many Austrians were hoping that it might bring an end to the crushing burden of unemployment and therefore adopted a positive or wait-and-see attitude. The rest of the population, the 'silent majority', expressed no opinion. This was due less to the presence of the German *Wehrmacht* than to the prompt intervention of the *Gestapo*, which had arrived in Vienna even before the military occupation and had immediately begun its fateful activities throughout Austria. Approximately sixty thousand Austrians, including all the political leaders, were arrested; some escaped abroad. At the same time the property of Austria's Jewish population was being confiscated, though initially the Jews were still able to emigrate. Many of them, unwilling to leave their native land at any price, failed to seize this opportunity and were to face an even more uncertain fate.[2] At first the new regime made a point of cultivating public opinion, but as the process of Nazification spread to all spheres of public life less and less attention was paid to it.

The Austrian federal provinces were transformed into *Gaue* with a number of boundary changes and the name Austria was intended to disappear entirely from the language. Key positions in public life were filled by Germans. Hitler, who had promised Mussolini that he would never forget his attitude during the *Anschluss*, signed on 21 October 1939 an agreement with Italy providing for the emigration of the people of the South Tyrol from their ancient homeland.

In September 1938 the great powers took another step forwards in their policy of appeasing Hitler, for at the Munich Conference they awarded the Sudetenland to National-Socialist Germany. Only the German annexation of the remainder of Czechoslovakia on 15 March 1939 led to a final change in public opinion in Britain and France. The German attack on Poland on 1 September 1939 finally started the Second World War.

A deep depression and sense of bewilderment descended on the Austrian population, who now had to live in a state that was about to start a murderous war with a large part of the world.

The fact that no government-in-exile was formed proved to be a considerable disadvantage to Austria. Attempts along these lines were foiled by the German advance into France. But, more importantly, the *émigrés*, representing a number of diametrically opposite political views, were unable to agree on a common line. Thus the Austrian people lacked moral support even from without. The majority of them had to take part in the war in the ranks of the German *Wehrmacht*. Characteristically, there was a total absence of the enthusiasm for war that had marked the mobilization of the Austrian imperial army in 1914. People accepted the inevitable, especially as many opponents of the Nationalist-Socialist regime felt less exposed to political persecution within the *Wehrmacht* than they would at home. In order to prevent the formation of centres of resistance there were hardly any compact Austrian units in the German *Wehrmacht* and instead Austrians were divided up among the national German regiments. It was one of the human tragedies of that terrible period that many Austrians now had to lose their lives for a political ideology that they had rejected all their lives.

In December 1941 Stalin first raised the subject of the restoration of Austria with Anthony Eden. On 18 February 1942 Winston Churchill declared that Britain did not recognize Austria's incorporation into the German Reich, and 19 October 1943 saw the opening of the Moscow conference of foreign ministers – Hull, Molotov and Eden – which produced the 'Moscow declaration' on the restoration of a free and independent Austria (1 November). The conference also decided to set up a European advisory commission which would work out proposals for the reorganization of Europe and also give aid to Austria after the collapse of Germany. The Moscow declaration ran as follows:

The Governments of the United Kingdom, the Union of Soviet Socialist Republics, and the United States have agreed that Austria, the first free country to fall a victim to Nazi aggression, shall be liberated from German domination. They regard the annexation imposed upon Austria by Germany's penetration on March 15 [correctly 13 March], 1938, as null and void. They consider themselves as in no way bound by any changes effected in Austria since that date. They declare that they wish to see re-established a free and independent Austria, and thereby to open the way for the Austrian people themselves, as well as those neighbouring States which will be faced with similar problems, to find that political and economic security which is the only basis for lasting peace. Austria is reminded, however, that she has a responsibility which she cannot evade for participation in the war on the side of Hitlerite Germany, and that in the final settlement, account will inevitably be taken of her own contribution to her liberation.

The Moscow declaration was to provide a positive signpost to Austria's future, but its reference to Austria's own contribution to liberation from National Socialism also raised many problems. Unfortunately the sacrifices that Austria made in the struggle against the National-Socialist regime have not found the recognition they deserve. Resistance groups[3] of the most varied political hues were first set up in Austria as early as 1938. But as the actions of these groups were not co-ordinated they lost a great many members without being able to operate effectively. Not until the last years of the war was there any active co-operation between them. And even then a great many Austrian resistance fighters had to sacrifice their lives or suffer in concentration camps. It was in these camps that like-thinking men, including some who were to become leading politicians of the Second Republic, succeeded in surmounting the old obstacles between parties and ideologies and in establishing the first contacts for deciding Austria's future.

In the seemingly hopeless situation of the concentration camps there arose among the detained Austrians the faith in Austria's rebirth that in 1945 and the subsequent years gave the country the strength to tackle the reconstruction of the state in a purposeful manner and in the teeth of all obstacles. Those Austrians who had not been directly exposed to persecution but had experienced the horrors of war and of the National-Socialist regime came to appreciate the freedom and independence of their country. This was frequently especially true of those who had been in favour of the *Anschluss* before 1938.

In November 1944 Stalin and Churchill, meeting in Moscow, also considered the possibility of Austria's amalgamation with the Catholic part of southern Germany, but this produced no concrete results. Agreement was reached on zones of occupation within Austria's frontiers and the plan contained in the Moscow declaration was upheld.

This solution was again approved at Yalta (4–5 February 1945), but when the Allied troops actually entered Austria no detailed plans had been drawn up concerning the occupation. The Yalta declaration merely spoke of the establishment of democratic institutions freely chosen by the nations of Europe liberated from German overlordship. Allied help was to be provided for the restoration of peaceful conditions, the mitigation of hardships, the setting up of provisional governments on broad democratic foundations and the holding of elections.

4

THE END OF THE WAR:
A NEW START

On 28 March 1945 Soviet troops crossed the Austrian frontiers and on 6 April the fighting reached the urban area of Vienna. On 9 April *Pravda* carried an appeal to the Austrian population restating the Soviet government's endorsement of the Moscow declaration of 1943. Thanks to the fact that the Austrian resistance movement was collaborating with the Soviet army, total destruction of Vienna's cultural treasures was avoided. But even so the week-long clash between the Soviet troops and the remnants of the German army in the urban area of Vienna caused considerable destruction in the districts where American bombing raids had not already done their work.

On 7 May military operations in Austria were suspended. Most of the German troops disengaged from the Soviet formations they were facing and surrendered to the American forces entering the country from the west and advancing from Bavaria into the Tyrol, Salzburg and Upper Austria. The British, moving up from Italy, occupied Carinthia at the same time. The Red Army advanced as far as the river Traisen, where it met the Americans.

Dr Karl Renner, who in 1945 was seventy-five years old, was staying at Gloggnitz on the Semmering when the Soviet army arrived. There he made contact with Soviet officers. On 17 April Renner arrived in Vienna – anxious to avoid the impression of acting on Soviet orders – and began his efforts to set up a provisional Austrian state government.

Vienna's reawakening political life was concentrated to begin with on the resistance leaders assembled at the Auersberg Palace and on the few prominent prewar politicians such as Theodor Körner, Dr Adolf Schärf and Leopold Kunschak who were in Vienna. Soon the old parties re-emerged. On 17 April the Austrian People's Party was founded by former Christian-Socialist politicians. Their leaders were members of the resistance movement (Gruber, Hurdes, Weinberger) and former concentration-camp inmates (Figl, Gorbach). When the Social Democrat Party was re-established under the name of the Socialist Party of Austria the representatives of its right wing (Renner, Schärf, Helmer) were the principal figures. An unknown quantity was the Communist Party, whose illegal leadership – men who had remained in Austria – was swiftly replaced by *émigrés* brought in from Moscow (Fischer, Koplenig and Honner, the latter having commanded Austrian units in Tito's army).

RESUMPTION OF POLITICAL ACTIVITY

On 27 April a provisional state government was formed under Karl Renner, with ten representatives from the Socialist Party, nine from the People's Party, seven Communists and three independents. Renner realized that the Communists were over-represented but he had to make allowances for the circumstances. On the same day the Democratic Republic of Austria was re-established by proclamation and the *Anschluss* was declared null and void. The provisional state government took up where the parliamentary system that preceded the establishment of the corporative state had left off. This was done by way of the government's constitutional continuity law of 1 May 1945, which brought the constitution of 1929 as well as all the constitutional laws on the statute book on 5 March 1933 back into force. A provisional constitution was adopted and was to apply until the first general elections were held and a new National Assembly was convened. The western powers did not at first recognize the Renner cabinet. The government's administrative power was therefore confined, for the time being, to the Soviet-occupied areas (Vienna, Lower Austria, Burgenland and Styria). The Soviet Union supported the provisional government in its endeavours to bring conditions in Austria back to normal and to get civilian life moving again. Yet the establishment of a unified military government for the whole of Austria was being delayed by the Soviets.

Difficult negotiations were necessary before the first control agreement could eventually be signed on 9 July. Towards the end of August units of the western occupying powers entered Vienna.

In Carinthia an executive committee had been formed after the entry of the British, and in July a provisional provincial government was established. In the Tyrol Dr Karl Gruber, heading a committee consisting of resistance leaders, had received American support as chief of the provincial administration on 3 May. Eventually Austrian provincial governments were also set up in the provinces of Salzburg and Upper Austria.

Renner tried to bring about a conference of all the Austrian federal provinces. His efforts were crowned with success on 25 September, when the first nation-wide conference of provinces took place in Vienna. At first there was a clash of opposing views, with Dr Gruber vigorously supporting the western point of view. Eventually agreement was reached on enlarging the provisional state government to thirteen representatives of the People's Party, twelve Socialists, ten Communists and four independents. The Allied council approved the formation of this government and recognized its authority over the whole of Austria. The Austrian Republic had risen again, with continuity under international law. On 25 November elections were held for the National Assembly and the provincial assemblies. The Austrian People's Party polled 1.6 million votes (85 seats) and the Socialist Party of Austria 1.4 million (76 seats), while the Communist Party of Austria suffered a defeat by polling only 174,000 votes (4 seats).

The first government, under Leopold Figl, with Dr Adolf Schärf as vice-chancellor, was made up of eight representatives of the People's Party, seven Socialists, two independents and one Communist.

The first few years of the Second Republic were characterized by the struggle against the famine and hardships of the postwar period. There was little scope for foreign policy, since the foremost task was to satisfy the population's immediate needs. The problems needing to be solved at this time seemed downright insoluble. A large amount of residential accommodation, transport installations and means of production had been destroyed. Hundreds of thousands of Austrians had lost their lives in military operations or were in captivity. Above all, Austria had become the direct sphere of influence of the four great powers, which had divided the country into four occupation zones. The efforts of the government and the people were therefore focused on preserving the unity of the country. The successful achievement of this aim seemed to many people a miracle. What had made this success possible was Austria's policy of self-assertion at home and abroad. But such an attitude was brought about only by the fact that – in contrast to 1918 – the desire for independence sprang from genuine conviction and that the overwhelming majority of Austrians now firmly rejected any association with Germany.

Moreover the threat that the country might be divided into an eastern half occupied by Soviet troops and a western half occupied by the western powers did much to weld all Austrians into a genuine community for better or worse. At home the awareness that any such tendencies had to be opposed gave them, even at this moment of material and physical weakness, an astonishing strength and unity. The most immediate and most ardent wish of everyone was, naturally enough, the withdrawal of the occupation troops of the four great powers and the full restoration of Austria's sovereignty. This was to be achieved only by political agreement. Since Austria had never been in a state of war with the occupying powers such an agreement could not be a peace treaty but solely an international treaty providing the basis for the country's full sovereignty. Among the statesmen of the Second Republic Karl Renner and Leopold Figl, thanks to their efforts during the first few postwar years, have become in the mind of the Austrian people the symbols of her struggle for unity, sovereignty and independence.

But what were Austria's chances in 1945 of achieving this aim of an international treaty? The success of any initiative in the field of foreign policy depended on the political situation in Central Europe. The Allies saw the solution of the problem – the withdrawal of the occupation troops – as being closely connected with other major decisions in Europe. Thus the deterioration of relations between the great powers and the beginning of the cold war greatly complicated Austria's endeavours.

It has repeatedly been claimed that Austria was unaware of the opportunities offered by her international status as a neutral and that Austrian neutrality stemmed from the specific international situation in 1955. Such a claim has not stood up to close examination.[1] It would of course be an over-simplification to explain the historical emergence of Austrian neutrality by distorting the facts. There is no doubt that the idea of neutrality, on what was then called the 'Swiss model', had been considered even between the two world wars. The necessary geographical conditions existed – the territory of Austria is situated in the heart of Central Europe and offers the most direct communications to her five neighbour states. This fact, together with the parallels between Austria and Switzerland, was discovered long before 1955. Karl Renner, for one, had formulated this idea very clearly a whole decade earlier.[2] The idea of a future neutral attitude had been repeatedly emphasized by leading Austrian politicians ever since 1945. It may be that these remarks occasionally failed to receive the attention they deserved from contemporary observers.

During the next few years Gruber, Körner and Gorbach frequently declared that Austria could not commit herself unilaterally, that neutrality was preferable to unilateral partisanship and that she did not propose to join any system of pacts. An international treaty that forced her to abandon her neutral attitude and to associate herself wholly with one power group or the other would be intolerable and unacceptable, declared Alfons Gorbach in his capacity as third president of the National Assembly.

As early as in his report to the provisional state government of 19 December 1945 – and subsequently as federal president – Karl Renner had pointed to Austria's efforts to achieve international protection for her sovereignty as an alternative to a policy of blocs. Instead of any further cementing of political alliances this proposal envisaged a solution very like neutrality. In April 1946 Renner declared that Austria could not commit herself unilaterally 'without upsetting the balance of interests'.[3] The first government statement of the Figl cabinet, of 25 November 1945, contained the same emphasis on a neutral position for Austria. This policy was expressed even more clearly in Figl's government statement after the elections in autumn 1949.

Between these two declarations of intent a great deal happened on the international scene in connection with the Austrian problem. From such sources as are at present available it is difficult to determine when exactly Allied contacts concerning the conclusion of a treaty with Austria began. Similarly, the background of progress and reverses in the lengthy negotiations necessarily remained largely hidden from view. As for the separate phases of the negotiations, these have been accurately analysed in publications by reputable experts – in so far as historians are able to do this today without access to the primary sources. Professor Gerald Stourzh of Vienna University distinguishes eight phases between 1945 and the signing of the treaty on 15 May 1955. He presents these under three headings – negotiations up to 1953, the emergence of the neutrality idea until 1953, and negotiations and the development of the concept of neutrality from 1953 to 1955.[4]

5

THE STRUGGLE FOR A TREATY

During the session of the Council of Allied Foreign Ministers in 1946 attempts were made to put the signing of a treaty with Austria on the agenda. In the summer of 1946 the 'examination of the Austrian question' was eventually discussed. In January 1947 the foreign ministers' deputies started to prepare a draft treaty,[1] and agreement was reached on roughly half of its articles. But it proved impossible to clear up the most important points, such as Yugoslavia's territorial demands, the question of German property and problems of de-Nazification. Although the federal chancellor was given an opportunity to present Austria's point of view in London,[2] Austria was far from being an equal partner in the negotiations.

The Moscow foreign ministers' conference of 10 March to 24 April 1947 revealed numerous differences between the western powers and the Soviet Union on the Austrian problem, especially on the issue of what was known as 'German property'. Although it had been decided at Potsdam (in July 1945) that no reparations would be exacted from Austria, 'German property' – which was in no way defined – in the Soviet occupation zone was to be handed over to the Soviet Union.[3] A commission appointed by the conference discussed the Austrian problem at numerous meetings but without success. After the equally unsuccessful foreign ministers' conference in London (November and December 1947) the Austrian problem was discussed by the Allied foreign ministers' deputies, but they too failed to reach a solution. The question of German property and the Yugoslav territorial claims on Austria proved particularly intractable.

One of the key questions of reconstruction and political alignment for all countries in postwar Europe was the decision on whether to participate in the Marshall Plan and the Organization for European Economic Co-operation (OEEC). It was a foregone conclusion that Austria would accept Marshall Plan aid and collaborate in OEEC. This was a vital *sine qua non* for the gigantic reconstruction tasks facing her after the destruction wrought by the war.

The establishment of NATO in April 1949 and the Berlin blockade were unmistakable symptoms of an increasing bloc formation in Europe. It was all the more vital for Austria to emphasize her independent position outside all blocs, and this was done in Figl's government statement of 1949. (The extent to which international problems were interlinked with the Austrian issue was again revealed – for once to Austria's advantage – when grave differences arose between the Soviet Union and Yugoslavia, leading to Tito's exclusion from the eastern bloc.) The effect became obvious at the Paris conference of foreign ministers in May and June 1949, when basic agreement was reached on vital points. Above all, the Soviet Union no longer supported the Yugoslavs' territorial demands. Austria's frontiers on 1 January 1938 were to remain inviolate. On the basis of economic concessions by Austria to the Soviet Union (150 million US dollars, 60 per cent of crude oil production, mining rights and refineries),[4] agreement was eventually reached on the outlines of the treaty that was to be signed. The four foreign ministers' deputies were instructed to work out a draft treaty during the next two months, but no agreement was reached on the economic issues.

The Paris conference decided that negotiations should be continued, but these (held in London from 4 July to 1 September and in New York in September) once again produced only partial results. In 1950 and 1951 the negotiations finally ground to a halt, after more than 250 sessions. In order to get the talks going again the western powers worked out in 1952 an 'abbreviated version' of the treaty, achieved by the simple expedient of deleting all points limiting Austria's sovereignty. This 'abbreviated treaty' was, however, rejected by the Soviet Union.

Of particular importance in this connection was the parliamentary debate of April 1952. At a moment when the Soviet Union had just rejected the western proposals for an abbreviated

treaty, Austria's future political position as a neutral under international law was clearly spelt out by the federal government
before the Austrian National Assembly.[5]

In the summer of 1952 the federal government submitted a
memorandum to all countries with whom Austria had diplomatic
relations, demanding an end to the occupation, the restoration of
Austria's sovereignty and the acceptance of the abbreviated version of the treaty.[6] The countless meetings of the foreign
ministers' deputies had aroused justified fears that negotiations
might come to a total standstill.

Simultaneously, with help from Brazil, the federal government
was seeking the support of the United Nations for getting negotiations on the treaty moving again. In December 1952 the UN
General Assembly, with no vote against and only two abstentions, passed a resolution holding the Allies responsible for the
restoration of a sovereign Austria in line with the Moscow
declaration of 1943.[7] But the General Assembly's resolution and
the subsequent exchange of notes produced no results at all.

The next step in Austria's efforts to get the treaty negotiations
off the ground was taken in the summer of 1953 by the Raab
government, which had been in office since 2 April. On 25 June
the foreign minister, Karl Gruber, had a meeting in Switzerland
with the Indian prime minister, Jawaharlal Nehru, in order to
request him to act as mediator. The Indian ambassador to
Moscow, Krishna Menon, was also present at this secret meeting.
Gruber asked Nehru for India's good offices in Austria's efforts
to encourage the Soviet Union to be more favourably disposed to
the idea of her military neutrality. Some time later Menon did in
fact point out to Molotov, the Soviet foreign minister, that
Austrian military neutrality could provide the basis for signing
the treaty. Molotov is thought to have pointed out that a declaration of neutrality was certainly useful but not sufficient.[8] Even
though this Austrian initiative, which remained secret for a long
time, did not at first produce any results it was undoubtedly of
great importance to the subsequent course of the negotiations.

It was therefore the Austrian federal government that
introduced the idea of neutrality in connection with the negotiations for the treaty. Thus the assertion that Austria accepted
neutrality only because she was forced to do so in 1955, at the
suggestion of one of the partners in the discussions, cannot be

c

upheld. Moreover Austria's offer of permanent neutrality was not a reckless renunciation of her sovereignty. The efforts of 1953 were concerned solely with the obligation of military neutrality, to be achieved not by way of an international treaty but through a unilateral declaration by Austria, i.e. a sovereign act by Austria. In this way any interference in Austrian affairs by the great powers was to be avoided. It is significant that an extensive and at times very lively debate about the concept of neutrality and its restriction to the field of international law had taken place in the Austrian parliament a year before. In addition to their contacts with the occupying powers, Austrian politicians had also engaged in lively international exchanges of ideas and were anxious for Austria to collaborate in international organizations. This anxiety was motivated by the wish to see Austria's international position strengthened by membership of these organizations and in this way to underline the independent position of the federal government, in spite of the existence of Allied special powers.[9]

Above all, Austria was interested in the United Nations. Full membership was not of course possible before the signing of the treaty. But with the second control agreement of the occupying powers for Austria in June 1946, membership and co-operation had become possible at least in relation to the specialized agencies of the United Nations, and she was readmitted to the former organizations within the League of Nations in which her membership had merely become dormant.[10] These were the International Telecommunications Union (1945), the World Postal Union (1946) and the International Labour Organization (1947). By 1948 Austria had become a member of ten international organizations.

Bilateral contacts in the field of foreign policy were also vigorously cultivated. Thus the federal chancellor met the Finnish premier, Urho Kekkonen, for an exchange of views in August 1953. Early in 1954 the great powers took the now historic step of breaking the ice of the cold war. After a pause of several years the foreign ministers of the four great powers – John Foster Dulles, Georges Bidault, Anthony Eden and Vyacheslav Molotov – once more sat round the same conference table in Berlin. The agenda included the Austrian question and for the first time representatives of the Austrian government –

the foreign minister, Figl, and the state secretary, Kreisky – participated as equal partners in the negotiations whenever these concerned Austria.

On 12 February – the first day of the talks devoted to the Austrian issue – Figl pointed out to the conference that, in spite of seven years of efforts, Austria was still waiting for the restoration of her sovereignty, even though in 1938 she had been the first victim of Germany's policy of aggression. Nevertheless Austria was ready to make financial sacrifices for the restoration of her freedom, provided such sacrifices were compatible with her economic capacity and with full economic sovereignty.[11]

The proposals tabled by Molotov the same day revealed that the fact that Austria's previously expressed willingness to adopt military neutrality had not failed to make an impression. The Soviet proposals involved prohibiting Austria's participation in any military alliances directed against the Allies of the Second World War. They further demanded a prohibition of foreign military bases as well as measures against any annexation of Austria to West Germany. This quasi-neutral status was to be imposed on the country by the occupying powers instead of being freely proclaimed by Austria. The differences concerning Austria's future international status and economic problems no longer seemed insoluble, especially as Molotov declared himself ready to accept compensation not in US dollars but in supplies of Austrian goods. On the other hand, these Soviet proposals were invalidated by Molotov's insistence that Allied troops should continue to remain in Austria, even after the conclusion of the treaty, until such time as the German issue had been settled – in other words, indefinitely. This the Austrian government refused to accept.

On 14 February the American secretary of state, John Foster Dulles, declared himself ready to accept all outstanding points of the 1949 version of the treaty, in the meaning of the Soviet version, and to sign the treaty within four days, i.e. by 18 February. Eden and Bidault supported the proposal, but the Soviet foreign minister, said to have been very much taken by surprise,[12] insisted on the proposals tabled by the Soviet side during the present conference. It is difficult to say whether the western powers had feared this reaction or hoped for it. At any rate Austria could not accept an arrangement that provided for the continued presence of the troops of the four powers on her territory unless she had a decisive say on the date of their departure.

On the other hand, on 16 February Figl made the first official government declaration on the avoidance of alliances: 'The Austrian people desire to live in peace and friendship with all states. Moreover, I am able to repeat here in all due form the statement of the federal government and the Austrian National Assembly to the effect that Austria has no intention of entering into any military alliances whatsoever.'[13] Dr Kreisky reports[14] that this declaration was by no means generally approved by the western powers. Molotov welcomed it as a step in the right direction but described it as not going far enough. A genuine solution was wrecked solely by the issue of the withdrawal of Allied troops. It was thus not so much the problem of Austria's future international position or that of payments to the Soviet Union that prevented agreement, but the Soviet Union's desire to wrap up the solution of the Austrian and the German issues in a single package.

The negotiations in Berlin had led to a far-reaching narrowing of the gap between opposing points of view and this outcome could be described as a partial success. On the other hand there was considerable disappointment over the fact that the problem had once more defied solution. Among ordinary Austrians the belief was increasingly gaining ground that the presence of occupation troops would have to be accepted as permanent.[15] At any rate the conference did not produce a treaty that would have been substantially less favourable to Austria than the one actually signed the following year, in 1955.

AFTER TEN YEARS – SUCCESS

The perseverance with which the Austrian delegation in Berlin, or indeed the Austrian federal government, had refused to accept a half-solution was to bear rich fruit within a year. Meanwhile yet another of the many 'arid' periods that occurred while they were endeavouring to achieve a treaty had to be survived.

Needless to say, the disappointing outcome of the Berlin conference was not received without comment in Austria. In particular the question of the country's future international status was again discussed in detail. In a debate in the National

Assembly shortly after the Berlin conference, Dr Gorbach referred to the Austrian point of view, accurately outlined on repeated occasions and most recently in Berlin, that no military alliances would be entered into in future. However, in Berlin Figl had refused to include an article to this effect in the text of the treaty. The aim of Austria's foreign policy was not neutralization from outside but neutrality freely chosen by the sovereign decision of the Austrian parliament. Besides, Austria was anxious to have this neutrality confined to the spheres of international law and military affairs. That is why Dr Gorbach, speaking in the debate in parliament, resisted the formulation, contained in the Soviet proposal, of 'no coalitions or military alliances of any kind'. Such a formulation could possibly be aimed against Austria's political and economic co-operation with foreign countries.[16]

Nearly a year passed without any likelihood of a treaty emerging. The year 1954 was more eventful as far as the political situation in Europe generally went. The desire to reduce the tension of the cold war on the one hand, and the integration of the Federal Republic of Germany into the western defence system on the other left their mark on the international situation.

In August 1954 the European Defence Community collapsed because of its rejection by the French Chamber of Deputies, but in spite of this setback the Paris treaties were drafted in a very short space of time. The Federal Republic of Germany was to become a member of Nato. The Western European Union was created as a substitute for the abortive European Defence Community. Towards the end of December 1954 the appropriate treaties were approved by the French Chamber and in February 1955 the German *Bundestag* voted its approval. The debate in the French Senate was scheduled for March.[17]

It was at this stage that the Supreme Soviet met, on 8 February 1955. According to Tass the session accepted the resignation of Malenkov, who was replaced, at Khrushchev's suggestion, by Bulganin. Molotov delivered a report on the international situation and on Soviet foreign policy, during which he made the following statement on the Austrian issue:

The Soviet Union attaches great importance to the settlement of the Austrian question, the question of the complete restoration of the independence of a democratic Austria in accordance with the interests of maintaining and strengthening peace in Europe.

The Soviet Government considers any further delay in the conclusion of a State Treaty with Austria to be unjustified. At the same time, one cannot fail to take into account the dangers involved in the plans to remilitarize Western Germany under the Paris Agreements.

All this leads the Soviet Government to draw the following conclusions with regard to the Austrian question:

(1) It is necessary first and foremost to reckon with the fact that the settlement of the Austrian question cannot be considered apart from the German problem, particularly in view of the plans to remilitarize Western Germany, which intensifies the danger of an *Anschluss*.

In concluding a State Treaty for Austria, such a solution must be found which would preclude the possibility of Germany carrying out a new *Anschluss*, which involves the taking of appropriate agreed measures by the four Powers on the German question. In this event the withdrawal of the troops of the four Powers from Austria could be carried out without waiting for the conclusion of a peace Treaty with Germany.

(2) Austria must undertake not to join any coalitions or military alliances directed against any Power that took part with its armed forces in the war against Hitler Germany and in liberating Austria, and not to permit the establishment of foreign military bases on her territory.

The USA, Britain, France and the Soviet Union must similarly undertake to carry out these provisions.

(3) For the earliest settlement of the Austrian issue a Four Power Conference must be called without delay to examine the German problem, as well as the question of concluding a State Treaty with Austria. Naturally this presupposes Austria's participation in the solution of the question of the Austrian State Treaty.

It should, however, be borne in mind that in the event of the ratification of the Paris Agreements, which open the way for the resurgence of militarism in Western Germany, a serious danger of an *Anschluss* would be created and consequently a threat to Austria's independence.[18]

The Soviet demand for an immediate four-power conference to discuss the German and Austrian issue was in line with the foreign policy pursued until then by the Soviet Union. Molotov's speech of 8 February would not therefore have caused any particular surprise over the Austrian question had it not been for the hint it contained that the question might after all, in certain circumstances, be discussed separately from the German question. Molotov's speech therefore produced a considerable stir in Austria. Western observers were divided in their views, while the western powers were sceptical. The Austrian government was not sure at first whether Molotov's formulations, which had been couched in very general terms, represented tactical concessions or a genuine concession, i.e. a waiver of the further occupation of Austria on certain conditions. The government therefore requested additional clarification of Molotov's remarks via the Soviet ambassador in Vienna.[19]

However, it turned out that such clarification was not so easy to obtain, though Austro-Soviet contacts did show that the hopes placed in Molotov's remarks of 8 February were justified. Molotov's statement was the prelude to a Soviet foreign policy initiative that was to prove of decisive significance for the restoration of Austria's sovereignty. The diplomatic activity embarked on by the Soviet government was altogether far more varied than many Western observers realized at the time.

On 25 February the Austrian ambassador in Moscow, Norbert Bischoff, was asked to call on Molotov, who repeated and underlined the importance of his remarks of 8 February – that the signing of the treaty and the withdrawal of Allied troops from Austria were possible even before the conclusion of a peace treaty with Germany, provided that satisfactory guarantees were provided against any new *Anschluss* with Germany. In the course of this lengthy conversation it also became clear that the solution of the German question was no longer seen by the Soviets as an indispensable prerequisite for the Austrian treaty, in particular so far as the withdrawal of Soviet troops from eastern Austria was concerned. During another meeting, on 2 March 1955, Bischoff informed Molotov that Austria was just as interested in finding means of reliably preventing a renewed *Anschluss* as the Soviet Union. On behalf of the Austrian government Bischoff asked for early Soviet proposals on this point. Molotov for his part asked for a concrete statement by the Austrian government on the various points made in his declaration on Austria of 8 February.[20]

On 14 March Bischoff handed Molotov the statement he had requested in the form of a 'Three-point declaration' by the Austrian government. In this they noted with satisfaction that the Soviet Union regarded as unjustified any further delay in the conclusion of a treaty with Austria. The three points of the declaration ran as follows:

(1) The Federal Government welcomes every effective assurance and guarantee of Austria's independence and freedom on all sides, and thus welcomes every effective assurance and guarantee against the danger of an *Anschluss*.

(2) The Federal Government has repeatedly and unequivocally declared that Austria has no intention of entering into military alliances or of permitting any military bases upon her territory. The Federal Government is ready to make the form in which any such declaration might eventually be given afresh the subject of an exchange of views.

(3) The Federal Government is also convinced that a final solution of the Austrian question can be reached only through a conference of all the Powers involved, with Austria also taking part. It considers nevertheless that the problems referred to under paragraphs (1) and (2) should be so clarified that such a conference would have prospects of speedy and concrete results.

The Federal Government believes that a successful result could be reached if the State Treaty were dealt with by the Four Powers, with Austria taking part, as a separate problem.

The declaration ended:

The matter is at present in the stage of an exchange of views designed to clarify opinions on both sides concerning the roads which might lead to a satisfactory solution of the problem affecting Austria.[21]

This of course simply meant that Austria did not favour the Soviet wish for a conference of the great powers to be summoned immediately but preferred to await proposals concerning the kind of guarantee to be given for Austria's independence. The Soviet reply to the 'three-point declaration' was bound to be of decisive importance to the success of the negotiations for a treaty.

The Swedish ambassador in Vienna, Sven Allard, has reported[22] that at a luncheon given by state secretary Kreisky, a conversation was held with the Soviet minister in Vienna, Sergei Kudryavtsev, in the course of which 'guarantees against an *Anschluss*' were aired. In response to a quotation of the text of the agreement adopted by the Congress of Vienna on Switzerland's neutrality, Kudryavtsev suggested, to everybody's surprise, that this or a similar proposal might form the basis of further discussions of the Austrian treaty. However the text referred to – he added – would have to be supplemented by the stipulation of measures that the occupying powers would be entitled to take in the event of Austria's independence being threatened by West Germany. This suggestion was decisively rejected by his Austrian interlocutors, who remarked that the Austrian government could never concede to the occupying powers the right to decide whether the country's independence was being threatened. Even less could they accept an arrangement under which these powers would be entitled to reoccupy their zones without the approval of the Austrian government.

On 20 March 1955 the federal chancellor made a broadcast on the political situation. He referred to the exchange of notes between Austria and the Soviet Union and pointed to Article 4 of the draft treaty, which prohibited an *Anschluss*. If further guarantees were considered necessary then it was up to the Soviet Union to submit the appropriate proposals. In the opinion of the chancellor the most suitable solution would be a joint guarantee of Austria's frontiers by the four occupying powers.[23]

On 24 March 1955 Molotov handed the Austrian ambassador in Moscow a note containing the Soviet government's positive reply to the Austrian note of 14 March. In it the Soviet government, in accordance with the wish of the Austrian government, declared itself ready to discuss the Austrian question separately from the German question at the conference that was to be convened. In addition to this Soviet concession a sensation was caused by Molotov's invitation to Raab to come to Moscow, accompanied by representatives of his own choosing, for the purpose of bilateral negotiations.

The western powers were at first exceedingly sceptical because of the connection that they suspected to exist between the wish to convene a four-power conference and the conclusion of the Paris agreements. Sven Allard points out that the Soviets felt that Austria should have exerted pressure on the western powers to call a four-power conference, as envisaged by the Soviets, at once – i.e. before the signing of the Paris agreements.[24]

Meanwhile the Soviet-Austrian exchange of notes was making further progress. By the end of March there was no doubt left in the minds of the western powers that the Soviet Union was seriously determined to bring about a restoration of Austria's full sovereignty and the withdrawal of the Soviet occupation troops independently of the conclusion of the Paris agreements.

On 29 March the Austrian Council of Ministers accepted the invitation for Raab to go to Moscow and decided that he should be accompanied by the vice-chancellor, Dr Adolf Schärf, the foreign minister, Leopold Figl, and state secretary Dr Bruno Kreisky.[25]

On 4 April the western powers confirmed their full confidence in the decisions of the Austrian federal government and agreed to the delegation's trip to Moscow.[26]

THE AUSTRIAN GOVERNMENT'S DELEGATION IN MOSCOW

On 11 April the members of the Austrian delegation took off from the then Soviet military airfield of Vöslau near Vienna on a journey that promised to be a landmark in international politics and a historic event. The delegation's invitation to Moscow had increasingly moved towards the centre of world interest, as it was being viewed in conjunction with other major foreign policy initiatives by the Soviet Union.

To Raab, the head of the delegation, the invitation to Moscow meant the confirmation of a policy he had persistently pursued since the formation of his first cabinet in 1953, a policy stemming from Austria's foreign policy since 1945. Regardless of all the unwelcome consequences of the prolonged occupation, Austria's statesmen had been searching for new ways of improving relations with the Soviet occupying power. To this end Raab had taken various initiatives. Among these he had been anxious to maintain contact with the Soviet high commissioner in Austria both before and after the Berlin conference, since he had wanted to establish a common basis of discussion with the Moscow government. This was by no means easy, as to many Austrians this attitude was initially suspect. They accused Raab of tending towards servility to the Soviet Union. Oskar Pollak, the editor of the *Arbeiterzeitung*, formulated this criticism in a famous leading article under the headline 'Raab – nix gut!'

But events proved Raab right. The Soviets accepted him as a negotiations partner with firm principles, as a politician who might represent a different social order but in whom they could have confidence. This was also reflected in Khrushchev's unconventional address in the Kremlin, at the end of the Moscow negotiations, when – according to Walter Kindermann, the Austrian delegation's interpreter – he gave Raab this jocular advice: 'Follow my example and turn Communist. . . . But if I really can't convince you then for God's sake stay as you are!'

The Austrian delegation was received in Moscow with all due formality and personal courtesy. Following various introductory calls on Molotov and Bulganin, negotiations began on 12 April with the Soviet government delegation, which was headed by Molotov and deputy premier Anastasi Mikoyan, and consisted of ten delegates.

The talks themselves were essentially centred on one political and one economic question. The political question concerned the nature of the guarantees for making Austria a factor in European peace after the withdrawal of the occupation troops, and for preventing the country from becoming a military deployment area. The economic question concerned compensation for 'German property' in Austria. In the course of the negotiations, which were conducted right from the start in a friendly and businesslike atmosphere and were soon making good progress, the Soviet Union announced its approval of Austria's neutral position. The Austrian delegation's declaration of Austria's intention to adopt a neutral stance on the Swiss model carried such weight that the Soviet side declared that they were satisfied. There was no more talk now of writing neutrality into the actual treaty, as had been demanded by Molotov as recently as at the Berlin conference. This in itself ensured a favourable outcome for the Moscow negotiations. Among other things the Soviet Union declared itself ready to sign the treaty without delay and to withdraw all occupation troops from Austria by 31 December 1955 at the latest.

The economic negotiations with Mikoyan ran into greater difficulties. But in this sphere, too, the Soviet Union was prepared to make major concessions, for political reasons.

Agreement was reached on the following Austrian obligations: ten million tons of petroleum over ten years, and two million US dollars for the DDSG (the Danube Shipping company) assets in Eastern Austria (the DDSG assets in Hungary, Rumania and

Bulgaria were to go to the USSR); for the USIA (Soviet-owned) enterprises in Austria the Soviet Union was to receive supplies of goods to the value of 150 million US dollars over six years.[27]

The results of the Moscow negotiations were recorded in the Moscow Memorandum of 15 April 1955. There has been some discussion about the nature of this memorandum. Professor Alfred Verdross, an international law expert in Vienna, pointed out that this was a 'political arrangement between the Soviet government and the Austrian government delegation'. It placed no obligation on the Republic of Austria but only on the members of the Austrian government delegation to see to it that certain measures were introduced.[28] It was thus a declaration of intent by the Austrian government delegation. Its historical and legal significance lay in the fact that it represented the first of 'a series of measures and decisions' that have since led to the acknowledgment of Austria's permanent neutrality.[29]

The key passage on Austria's neutrality in the Moscow Memorandum states that the members of the Austrian government delegation,

> ...in connection with the decision on the Austrian treaty will see to it that the following decisions and measures are adopted by the Austrian federal government.
>
> In the spirit of Austria's declaration—first made at the Berlin conference in 1954—that she would enter into no military alliances and would not permit the establishment of military bases on her territory, the Austrian federal government will make a declaration in a form that would impose upon Austria the international obligation always to observe a neutrality such as is observed by Switzerland....[30]

Following the Austrian delegation's return to Vienna there was an exchange of notes between the Soviet Union and the western occupying powers. On 19 April the Soviet Union proposed that a conference of the 'big four' foreign ministers should be held in Vienna. The western powers agreed to this but favoured a preliminary conference of the ambassadors accredited in Vienna to prepare the ministers' meeting. This ambassadors' conference, at which Austria was represented by Figl and Kreisky, first met on 2 May. A few stipulations that were onerous for Austria were deleted from the text of the treaty but a serious controversy arose on the subject of 'German property' and other economic matters;

however, this was settled by a compromise on 12 May. On 14 May the foreign ministers of the four occupying powers – Dulles, Macmillan, Pinay and Molotov, the latter being in the chair – met for joint negotiations with Figl. In these talks a final amendment to the text of the treaty, to meet Austria's wishes, was agreed on. This concerned the deletion of the passage in the preamble which referred to Austria bearing a certain degree of responsibility for the events of the war.[31] The communiqué on the conference, dated 14 May 1955, reveals that the three western foreign ministers raised no objections to the road mapped out in the Moscow Memorandum. As for Austria's future neutrality, however, they proposed to await the passing of the appropriate statute by the Austrian parliament.[32] At Austria's suggestion the signing of the treaty was eventually fixed for Sunday, 15 May, at the Belvedere Palace in Vienna.

This was possibly the finest use to which this jewel of Baroque architecture, built for Prince Eugene of Savoy by Lukas von Hildebrandt, was ever put in the whole course of its eventful history. On 15 May 1955 the Austrian state treaty was solemnly signed in the Marble Hall of the Belvedere Palace by Vyacheslav Molotov, Harold Macmillan, John Foster Dulles, Antoine Pinay and Leopold Figl. A vast crowd filled the Belvedere Gardens when the foreign ministers of the four great powers stepped out on to the balcony of the palace with their Austrian colleague. Arms raised, Figl held out to his cheering compatriots the original of the signed treaty. It was a moment of joy at the manifest success of reason and it united the assembled crowd and the political leaders of the world in a unanimity of emotion, remaining indelibly engraved on the memories of all those present.

Following the signing of the treaty the five foreign ministers expressed their pleasure and satisfaction at what had been achieved. Dulles emphasized that it was Austria herself who had regained her freedom and independence. Molotov described the signing of the treaty as an important international event and a day of jubilation for the Austrian people; he emphasized that now that the Austrian question had been solved the Soviet Union would strive to see that the solution of the German question was not delayed any longer. Leopold Figl, in a statement full of joy and emotion, pointed out that the Austrians' faith in their future had borne fruit after seventeen difficult years.[33]

The conclusion of the Austrian treaty coincided with the reopening of the great cultural institutions destroyed during the war – the Burgtheater and the Vienna State Opera House. The moment at which their reopening took place gave these brilliant occasions a symbolic character which was accepted as such by the entire Austrian people. It was no coincidence that *Fidelio*, Beethoven's opera extolling freedom, had been chosen for the opening performance at the Opera House. The conductor was Karl Böhm. In the audience with their Austrian hosts were the political leaders of East and West as well as numerous friends of Austria who had come from all over the world to attend the performance.

Following its ratification and the deposition of the ratification documents the treaty came into force on 27 July 1955. The same day the Allied Council in Vienna dissolved itself and the ninety-day time limit for the withdrawal of the occupation troops began. On 25 October the last occupation soldier left Austria.[34] The following day the Austrian National Assembly passed the federal constitutional law concerning Austria's permanent neutrality.

The country's problems were not of course dramatically solved in 1955, but the Austrians were once more masters in their own house and were now able to make a start on remedying all omissions without interference.

THE BACKGROUND

The conclusion of the Austrian treaty and the resulting withdrawal of the occupation troops had seemed to many Austrians an unrealizable pipe-dream and to foreign observers altogether impossible. It therefore came to most people as a complete surprise. Politicians and commentators speculated on what had caused a sudden change of opinion in the Kremlin after ten years. It should also be mentioned that many western circles were not exactly enthusiastic about the treaty since they doubted whether Austria would be able to maintain her independence and sovereignty once the western occupation troops had been withdrawn. The Austrian federal government, however, had left no one in any doubt that they felt fully capable of ensuring Austria's independence and that they had full confidence in the loyalty of all the signatory powers.

In the absence of concrete evidence any attempt to find reasons for what happened in the Kremlin at that time must be based on surmise, but there is no doubt that the signing of the treaty must be viewed in the context of the international developments of the day. It is likely, for instance, that Khrushchev's takeover of government affairs resulted in a reassessment of past Soviet policy.

October 1954 saw the settlement of the Trieste issue, which meant that it was no longer possible to link it with the Austrian question. At about the same time came the conclusion of the London and Paris agreements, resulting in the establishment of the Western European Union (WEU) and in West Germany joining the North Atlantic Treaty Organization (Nato). Finally, the signing of the Warsaw Treaty in the spring of 1955 provided a new basis for the stationing of Soviet troops in the countries of the eastern bloc, and thus the justification that these troops had to stay in Hungary and Rumania in order to maintain communications with the Soviet troops in Austria was no longer valid.

International comment mentioned other reasons for the change in the Soviet attitude, including the suggestion that with the solution of the Austrian problem Moscow had wanted to set a pattern for the settlement of the German problem. But it seems rather unlikely that the Soviet leadership should have adopted such tactics at a time when West Germany had already decided to join the Nato alliance. On the other hand it is possible that some part was played by the consideration that Austria's neutral status would deny to Nato's strategic planning the central range of the Alps from Switzerland to their final spurs in eastern Austria.[35] It is certain that Khrushchev was in favour of signing the Austrian state treaty in spite of clear opposition from influential circles within the Soviet leadership. Indeed he made no secret of this in talks with Austrian politicians during his subsequent state visit to Austria. The signing of the treaty during a period of international *détente* finally marked the policy of peaceful coexistence pursued by the then Soviet Party leader and later premier. Moscow's assent to the Austrian state treaty was clearly designed to buttress the credibility of Khrushchev's policy of *détente*.

No doubt Austria's willingness to stay outside any system of pacts, i.e. to adopt a neutral status, made it easier for Khrushchev to surmount the difficulties that arose from the reserved attitude of senior party and military circles to the treaty and to the withdrawal of the Soviet occupation troops. Sven Allard, analysing these events in his memoirs, reaches a similar conclusion.[36] He says that two alternatives were open to the Kremlin at the time. They could use the Austrian example to demonstrate the Soviet Union's positive contribution to the policy of *détente*, and this example might at the same time serve as a model to other states in avoiding association with the two great power blocs or freeing themselves from existing ties. To this was added Moscow's anxiety lest with the rearmament of West Germany within the Nato framework the western occupation zones in Austria should be integrated within the defence system of the Atlantic Treaty. Such a development had been forestalled by the Austrian treaty and by a corresponding declaration of neutrality by Austria. The other alternative would have been the sealing-off of Austria's eastern zone and its gradual integration into the eastern bloc.

Discussions between the representatives of these two theses had apparently ended with Moscow's decision to attempt a settlement based on a voluntary declaration of neutrality by Austria. As soon as Austria's readiness to do so had been convincingly demonstrated by her government a decision had been taken in Moscow to sign the treaty. It is now known that the Soviet Union intended to sign the treaty as early as the Berlin conference. Khrushchev himself told Austrian interlocutors that Molotov had at that time held the view that they could support the treaty without sacrificing military positions.[37] When it turned out that Austria would not accept such a treaty the problem was re-examined in Moscow and Molotov's view was rejected. Khrushchev – on his own evidence – thought it more important to provide clear proof of his willingness to negotiate than to cling to less vital military positions.[38]

It therefore seems to have been realized in Moscow that Austria was prepared to accept only a treaty that contained no military obligations. To the Soviet leadership the decisive issue was therefore whether a satisfactory guarantee could be obtained against a renewed annexation of Austria to Germany. Thus the neutrality issue moved into the foreground of the discussions.

Ever since 1947 Austria's political leaders – Renner, Körner, Raab, Figl, Kreisky, Maleta and Gruber – had pointed out the usefulness of neutral status. It is impossible to overemphasize this fact, since it demonstrates the common foreign policy line of the two great constitutional parties of our country on this vital issue. Nothing in fact could be 'more fatal to Austria's existence as a free state than that the two great domestic camps should align themselves in opposition to each other over foreign policy'.[39]

The question of neutrality had been repeatedly raised in discussions of foreign policy between 1945 and 1955. Early in 1947 the federal president, Dr Karl Renner, wrote in an article in the *Wiener Zeitung*: 'It has repeatedly been pointed out that the Austrian Republic claims for the future a similar role and destiny as the Swiss Confederation.' In 1951 the federal chancellor, Theodor Körner, had stated: 'A free, independent Austria, removed from all rivalries, not unilaterally tied in any direction, dedicated solely and exclusively to the cause of peace, will be an asset to Europe, to the world.' That same year Dr Alfred Maleta, for many years president of the National Assembly, asked in a speech 'how non-communist Austria could hope to receive a peace treaty from the premier communist world power?' He answered his own question by pointing out that only the road of strict neutrality in all directions held any chance of success.[40] On 30 October 1953 Maleta told the National Assembly: 'Austria therefore has a clear personal interest in pursuing a genuine policy of neutrality, in the sense that this concept has been traditionally understood by international law.'[41]

Although the statements of Austrian politicians did not at the time yield the hoped-for results, they nevertheless cleared the ground in the field of foreign policy for a subsequent solution and moreover prepared the Austrian public psychologically for the federal government's policy of neutrality. When the question eventually arose in concrete form in 1955 it was no longer new and could be solved with the full consent of all relevant political forces in the country.

The talks held by the Austrian government delegation in

Moscow in April 1955 showed that the Soviet government was quite ready to accept Austria's neutrality as a guarantee against a renewed *Anschluss* with Germany. No attempt whatever was made in Moscow to foist neutrality upon Austria.[42]

The signing of the treaty and the withdrawal of the occupation troops can therefore be explained by the simultaneous emergence of a number of favourable circumstances. Whereas the invitation to Moscow had been seen by many in the West as a tactical manoeuvre, the Austrian government had believed that the Soviet Union meant business. It is certainly to the credit of the men of the Austrian government team – Raab, Schärf, Figl and Kreisky – that they judged the situation correctly and drew the necessary conclusions at what was probably the only possible moment in time.

ॐ 6

AUSTRIA AND PERMANENT NEUTRALITY

'Permanent neutrality' has become the most essential factor of Austrian foreign policy. The neutral status of our country under international law is of such importance that it seems appropriate to touch on a few problems concerning it. To begin with, it should once more be emphasized that Austria's neutrality is in every way an obligation freely undertaken. The treaty contains no clauses or suggestions whatever involving an obligation on Austria's part to preserve her neutrality.

When we assess Austria's permanent neutrality we must remember that the Austrian people had first of all to get used to this new status. After all, from 1526 onwards Austria had been the nucleus of a great power and as such had been accustomed to living within a great and virtually self-sufficient political community. Professor Alfred Verdross is therefore quite right when he observes that it was only after some initial wavering that our people realized 'that they have an important European task to fulfil by their mere independent political existence as a state bounded by eastern Alps along their entire length and breadth'.[1] Undoubtedly it was the great powers' realization that the existence of an independent Austria was necessary for the maintenance of world peace that led to the Moscow declaration of 1 November 1943, according to which the annexation of Austria on 13 March 1938 would be regarded as null and void and in which a hope for the restoration of a free, independent Austria was voiced. This declaration eventually formed the basis of the Austrian government's efforts after 1945 to restore the country's independence.

The struggle for the treaty which gave Austria her full sovereignty has been described in the previous chapter. The breakthrough point in the efforts to achieve this treaty came in January 1954 at the Berlin conference of foreign ministers, when the Austrian delegation declared for the first time that Austria would not join any military pact or permit the establishment of military bases in Austria. Even though this declaration did not result in a decision by the foreign ministers' conference, it did nevertheless create the basis for the subsequent signing of the treaty. No doubt it also paved the way for the statement about Austria made by Molotov on 8 February 1955, from which it transpired that the neutrality offered by Austria at the Berlin conference would provide a suitable basis for an agreement.[2] The Moscow Memorandum of 15 April 1955 therefore represents the logical outcome of this development and may be seen as the first international document on Austria's permanent neutrality. It contains the following stipulations:

I. In the course of conversations regarding the earliest conclusion of the Austrian State Treaty in Moscow from the 12th to the 15th of April 1955 agreement was reached between the Soviet and the Austrian delegations that, with regard to the declarations made by the members of the Soviet Government—the Deputy Chairman of the Council of Ministers and the Minister for Foreign Affairs of the U.S.S.R., V. M. Molotov, and the Deputy Chairman of the Council of Ministers of the U.S.S.R., A. I. Mikoyan—Federal Chancellor Ing. Julius Raab, Vice-Chancellor Dr Adolf Schärf, Foreign Minister Dr. h.c. Ing. Leopold Figl, State Secretary Dr Bruno Kreisky in connection with the conclusion of the Austrian State Treaty will see to it that the following decisions and measures of the Austrian Federal Government are brought about:

1. In the sense of the declaration already given by Austria at the conference in Berlin in 1954 to join no military alliances and to permit no military bases on her territory, the Austrian Federal Government will make a declaration in a form which will obligate Austria internationally to practice in perpetuity a neutrality of the type maintained by Switzerland.

2. The Austrian Federal Government will submit this Austrian declaration in accordance with the terms of the Federal Constitution to the Austrian Parliament for decision immediately after ratification of the State Treaty.

3. The Federal Government will take all suitable steps to obtain

international recognition for the declaration confirmed by the Austrian Parliament.

4. The Austrian Federal Government will welcome a guarantee by the four great powers of the inviolability and integrity of the Austrian State Territory.

5. The Austrian Federal Government will seek to obtain from the Governments of France, Great Britain and the United States of America such a guarantee by the four great powers.

II. The Deputy Chairmen of the Council of Ministers, V. M. Molotov and A. I. Mikoyan, made the following declaration in the name of the Soviet Government with regard to the declarations of the Austrian Government delegation:

4. The Soviet Government is prepared to recognize the declaration concerning the neutrality of Austria.

5. The Soviet Government is prepared to participate in a guarantee by the four powers of the inviolability and integrity of the Austrian State Territory—according to the model of Switzerland.

In his report to the Austrian National Assembly on 27 April 1955 Julius Raab observed that the declaration on Austria's permanent neutrality, as envisaged in the Moscow Memorandum, was of special value only if it was 'made by a fully sovereign state. To extort such a declaration would only reduce its value.' The federal chancellor remarked that he had met with 'full understanding' of this view in Moscow.[3]

On 7 June the central executive of the National Assembly unanimously decided that the National Assembly would adopt the following resolutions:

With the object of the lasting and perpetual maintenance of her independence from without and the inviolability of her territory, as well as in the interest of maintaining internal law and order, Austria declares of her own free will her permanent neutrality, and is resolved to maintain and defend it with all means at her disposal.

Austria, in order to secure these objectives, will join no military alliances and will not permit the establishment of military bases of foreign states on her territory.

In this connection she declares her desire to observe at all times in her relations with other states the principles laid down in the United Nations charter, and once again voices her willingness and ability to accede to and observe the obligations contained in the charter.

The federal government is moreover requested to submit to the National Assembly the draft of a federal constitutional law regulating this neutrality, to take all steps to achieve eventual admission to the

United Nations organization, which has already been applied for, as soon as the Austrian state treaty has come into force and Austria has been evacuated by the occupation troops, and to inform all countries of this law, requesting them to recognize Austria's neutrality.[4]

After the withdrawal of the foreign occupation troops the Austrian National Assembly adopted the following constitutional law on 26 October 1955:

Article I: (1) With the object of the lasting maintenance of her independence from without and the inviolability of her territory, Austria declares of her own free will her permanent neutrality. She is resolved to maintain and defend it with all means at her disposal.

(2) In order to secure these objectives Austria will join no military alliances and will not permit the establishment of military bases of foreign states on her territory.

Article II: The federal government is entrusted with the implementation of this constitutional law.[5]

All states with whom Austria maintained diplomatic relations were notified of this law with a request that they should recognize Austria's permanent neutrality. This request was met by sixty-one countries – either expressly or by taking note without objection.

Although the Moscow Memorandum is regarded in some quarters as a treaty signed by Austria and the Soviet Union, the general legal view is nevertheless that it merely represents a political arrangement between the Soviet Union and the Austrian government delegation.[6] As Verdross points out, a treaty exists only

... when it endeavours by its content to establish international rights and duties. However, this does not apply to the Moscow Memorandum for the following reasons: to begin with the Austrian Government delegation was in no position to enter into any obligations concerning Austrian neutrality since under Article 50 of the Austrian federal constitution political state treaties can be entered into only by the federal president with the approval of the National Assembly. In addition, the text of the Moscow Memorandum does not impose duties upon the Austrian Republic but merely obliges the members of the Austrian government delegation to 'see to it' that certain measures are taken. Moreover, it states that the federal government will submit the 'declaration' to be formulated about neutrality to the Austrian parliament 'for a decision upon it', which again shows that the Moscow Memorandum is not a treaty binding upon the republic.

As Verdross quite correctly points out, this must not lead to the erroneous conclusion that the Moscow Memorandum is meaningless in law. On the contrary it forms the basis of the measures subsequently taken by the Austrian federal government and the National Assembly. It seems important to quote further from Professor Verdross's analysis:

> For this reason we cannot agree with those authors who maintain that the permanent neutrality of the Austrian Republic is anchored only in the neutrality law of 26 October 1955, and could therefore again be amended by our state, i.e. unilaterally. The error of this view already stems from the fact that the members of the Austrian government delegation undertook, under Point 1 of the Moscow Memorandum, to see to it that the Austrian declaration of neutrality was made in a form that would oblige Austria to maintain permanent neutrality of the kind practised by Switzerland on an international level. Since, however, the documents already quoted clearly show that both the Austrian federal government and the National Assembly intended faithfully to discharge the obligations of the Austrian government delegation as contained in the Moscow Memorandum, the measures adopted by them must be seen in that light. This would not be in any way different even if the Moscow Memorandum were a treaty under international law, considering that the federal government has already discharged all the obligations undertaken by it under Points 1 to 3. It should be added that the Austrian neutrality law by itself does not represent any obligation for the Austrian Republic under international law. These obligations have come into being only through the fact that the powers have either acknowledged or noted without objection the notification of the Austrian Republic's permanent neutrality.[7]

THE OBLIGATIONS ARISING FROM NEUTRALITY

As Austrian neutrality is intended, under the Moscow Memorandum, to follow the Swiss model, it seems appropriate, before dealing with the nature and extent of the obligations arising from Austria's neutrality, to list the rights and obligations of a permanently neutral state as they have emerged from Switzerland's legal development and continuous practice:

1. It [a permanently neutral state] is obliged to observe the norms

of neutrality under international law in all wars between other states.

2. It is, however, not only entitled but indeed obliged to defend its territory against attacks from outside with all means at its disposal. Permanent neutrality must therefore be armed neutrality.

3. Even in times of peace it must not enter into any obligations that might involve it in a war. This means that it must neither make alliances nor grant another state military bases on its territory, since in this way it might be involved in wars between other states. Moreover it must not enter into any obligations that would involve it in non-neutral behaviour, i.e. behaviour running counter to the rules of the common law of neutrality that comes into force only in wartime. Such obligations are known as 'secondary duties or anticipated effects of permanent neutrality'.

4. It is entitled, on the other hand, to solicit from other powers guarantees of the integrity of its state territory and to accept from them guarantee declarations.

5. In any other way it remains entirely free to shape its domestic and foreign policy as it chooses, in so far as it does not enter into any divergent contractual obligations.

6. In particular there is no obligation of ideological neutrality. The freedom of the press and of opinion is therefore not limited by permanent neutrality. Thus when some National Socialist writers demanded that the neutral states should also observe ideological neutrality, this demand was rejected not only by Switzerland but also by Norway as not justified in international law. Moreover, the freedom of the neutral press was expressly guaranteed by the Fifth Hague Convention on neutrality on land (1907).

It is therefore clear that a permanently neutral country must, even in peacetime, 'do everything to avoid being involved in a war and refrain from doing anything that might involve it in a war'. In other words it must conduct a 'policy of neutrality'. The shaping of such a policy in detail, however, is a matter for its own judgement within the limits set out under Point 3.[8]

The obligations arising from Austria's neutrality are clearly laid down in the constitutional law of 26 October 1955. Its interpretation, according to Verdross,[9] leads to the following conclusions.

The declaration that Austria will practise permanent neutrality implies that she will remain neutral in any war that may break out; this means that Austria must not, even in peacetime, enter into any obligations that would make it impossible for her, in the event of a war between other countries, to act in accordance with the norms of the law of neutrality as laid down in the Hague Convention of 18 October 1907 concerning neutrality on land and sea and in the common usage of international law.

One of the consequential obligations of a neutral country is that its territory must not be used by belligerents and that belligerent parties must not be supported, either by the supply of war materials or by loans for military purposes. The Hague Convention of 1907 also contains the stipulation that all restrictions and prohibitions imposed by a neutral power in respect of private military supplies (military supplies by states are prohibited) must be applied in equal measure to all belligerents.

Apart from these obligations a permanently neutral state can regulate its foreign trade policy as it pleases. Thus although there is no such thing as general economic neutrality, a permanently neutral state must not, even in peacetime, enter into any economic obligations that would make it impossible for it to discharge the obligations listed above in the event of war.

In this connection it is interesting to note that in both world wars Switzerland applied to its freight traffic with foreign countries the principle of *courant normal*, which means that it maintained a volume of trade in accordance with the scale of peacetime goods traffic. Admittedly there is no obligation under international law to act in this way.[10]

The constitutional law of 26 October 1955 further stipulates that Austria will maintain and defend her permanent neutrality with all the means at her disposal. From this it follows on the one hand that Austria must so conduct her foreign policy that she is not involved in any war, and on the other that she is obliged to defend her neutrality by force of arms if need be. Finally it contains the stipulation that even in peacetime Austria must not enter into any military alliances or permit the establishment of military bases by foreign states on her territory.

Austria's duties arising from her neutrality under international law are therefore substantially in line with the Swiss model. The government statement made in the National Assembly on 26 October expressly points out that the neutrality law 'in no way limits the basic rights and freedoms of citizens'. It further observes that 'neutrality is an obligation of the state but not of the individual citizen. The intellectual and political freedom of the individual, in particular the freedom of the press and of the free statement of opinion, are not affected by a country's permanent neutrality. It does not therefore entail any obligation to practise ideological neutrality.'

THE LAW OF NEUTRALITY AND A POLICY OF NEUTRALITY

The further development of neutrality and of new forms of international co-operation creates additional problems for a permanently neutral state. When neutrality first came into existence and the norms of the law of neutrality were created, certain aspects of present-day international relations were not yet present. Thus there were no supranational organizations, no League of Nations, no United Nations, and not even regional economic unions. It is therefore obvious that while the law of neutrality scarcely took these aspects into account at the time, today it cannot avoid doing so. In this context the difference between the law of neutrality and a policy of neutrality becomes increasingly important. The law of neutrality is the sum total of the international norms that impose certain obligations on a neutral state under international law. These include the duty to pursue a policy of neutrality within the framework outlined above. How such a policy is shaped is left to the judgement of the neutral country.

The law of neutrality, as laid down in particular in the Hague Convention, represents a common law applying to neutral countries – e.g. the principle of not entering into alliances or the principle of equal treatment for all belligerents in respect of supplies of goods of military importance. Logical conclusions necessarily arise from the law of neutrality for a country's policy of neutrality, but this, as we have said, is left to the judgement of each neutral state. It follows that even in peacetime a permanent neutral state must conduct its policy in such a way that the norms of neutrality are observed. But whereas the law of neutrality is the same for all neutral states, a policy of neutrality is governed by the geopolitical, economic and military conditions of the country concerned. Thus the law of neutrality is absolute while a policy of neutrality is relative. This is easily illustrated by a comparison of the policies of neutrality practised by Switzerland, Austria and Sweden. Switzerland, for example, is not a member of the United Nations, whereas Austria has joined the world organization. Switzerland no doubt decided against membership on the grounds of her experiences in the League of Nations, for when she joined the League she was exempted from military sanctions by decision of the League of Nations Council, but the Swiss Confederation accepted the obligation of non-military sanctions. This question became topical in connection with the Abyssinian conflict, when effective economic sanctions were voted against Italy. Switzerland withdrew her participation from non-military sanctions, realizing that participation would inevitably involve her in a warlike conflict.

For Austria the situation was different. Following the conclusion of the 1955 treaty the federal government applied for membership of the United Nations. In the preamble to the treaty the great powers had declared themselves ready to support Austria's application for admission to the United Nations, even though they knew that Switzerland was not a member. This revealed clearly that the Allied powers regarded membership of an international organization such as the United Nations as entirely compatible with the status of Austria's permanent neutrality. Following the signing of the treaty and the withdrawal of the last occupation soldiers the Austrian parliament, as we have seen, passed the federal constitutional law concerning permanent neutrality. This came into force on 5 November and all states with which Austria maintained diplomatic relations were notified of it. In December Austria's application for admission to the United Nations was accepted. The United Nations thereby accepted a state that was already permanently neutral at the time of admission. It follows that both the members of the Security Council and all states voting for Austria's admission in the General Assembly regarded her membership as entirely compatible with her neutral status. Thus Switzerland believed that she could preserve her neutrality better by not being subject to the obligations resulting from membership of the United Nations, while Austria, faced with a considerably more difficult geopolitical situation, took the view that membership would considerably strengthen her international position.

The attitudes of Switzerland and Austria to the Council of Europe also reflect their different concepts of a policy of neutrality. Whereas Austria joined the Council as early as 1956, Switzerland did not take this step until much later. Although the Swiss government never stated that membership was incompatible with the law of neutrality, they decided in favour of membership only when they regarded the moment as opportune and as fitting into their concept of neutrality.

Reference should also be made to relations with other regional communities of states such as the OECD, Efta and the EEC. Whereas the first two organizations are based on the classical principle of co-operation (i.e. unanimity), the same does not apply to the EEC, which represents a supranational institution with majority decisions and is intended to develop from a customs union into an economic union. Thus while it is perfectly possible for a neutral country to become a member of an organization in the first category, membership of one in the second category would be possible for a neutral state only under certain conditions, or on the basis of appropriate contractual arrangements with such an organization designed to preserve the neutral's full sovereignty. It could not therefore submit to any majority decisions of a group of states if these were to jeopardize its sovereignty. There is far-reaching agreement that a permanently neutral state cannot, in view of the provisions of the law of neutrality, be a full member of such a grouping of states; if it were it would run the risk, in the event of war, of being no longer able to discharge the obligations arising from its neutrality, since in view of its economic integration with the economic community it would not be in a position to take any independent decisions.[11]

During the consultations on the United Nations charter in San Francisco in 1945 there emerged a clear trend towards subordinating neutrality to collective security. It was in line with these considerations that the French delegate, Joseph Paul-Boncour, moved the inclusion in the charter of a specific stipulation to the effect that the status of neutrality would in future be incompatible with the charter and the obligations arising from it. He was clearly trying to prevent neutral states from evading the obligations arising from the charter by pointing to their neutral status. Although this motion was rejected by the Political Commission, the feeling was expressed that neutrality was incompatible with the United Nations charter.[12]

Nowadays, however, the general view is that true neutrality is entirely possible under the United Nations charter. As far as Security Council decisions under chapter VII of the charter are concerned, i.e. measures against a possible aggressor, these are binding on all states, while military measures require special agreements between the Security Council and each separate state. Admittedly the Security Council can waive such a demand – a point of particular importance to a neutral state. The members of the United Nations are not therefore obliged – as those of the League of Nations used to be – to take immediate and direct measures against an aggressor; before they embark on any action an appropriate resolution must be adopted by the Security Council.[13]

In point of fact the Security Council is not obliged to call upon all members for sanctions under chapter VII of the charter and may exempt certain states. How many states are in fact enlisted for such actions depends in each case on the decision of the Security Council.

As we have seen, participation in military sanctions, including the granting of the right of passage under article 43 of the charter, depends on a special agreement between the Security Council and the individual states. It is not therefore necessary for a neutral state to be formally exempted from the obligation of participation in such measures; it is sufficient for the Security Council not to make a special agreement under article 43, section 3 of the charter with states which it wishes to exempt from participation in military sanctions. It follows that United Nations membership of a neutral state is entirely compatible with neutrality. It is unlikely that the United Nations, who were notified of the constitutional law of 26 October 1955 on Austria's permanent neutrality, would call on neutral Austria to participate in military sanctions under chapter VII of the charter. It is unlikely, if only for the reason that the four great powers, as permanent members of the Security Council and as signatories to the Austrian treaty, sponsored Austria's admission to the United Nations in the preamble to the treaty. By doing so they expressed their belief that neutrality was compatible with membership of the United Nations; simultaneously they undertook the task of enabling Austria to preserve her obligations as a neutral within the framework of the United Nations.[14] Should such a call be received from the Security Council, Austria has the option of declining to make the agreement that, under article 43 of the charter, is necessary for participation in military sanctions. The fact is that since her admission to the United Nations in December 1955 Austria has never been confronted with this question – which is probably the best proof that this argument is a good one.

Non-military sanctions are not subject to such special agreement, which means that all member states are obliged to observe Security Council resolutions along such lines. At the same time, the Security Council is also entitled to exempt a country from participation in non-military sanctions. It follows therefore that there are no objections to the dispatch of Austrian units to foreign countries for peace-keeping operations provided a request to that effect has been addressed to Austria by the United Nations. In line with this interpretation Austria has repeatedly participated in such operations, for instance in the Congo and in Cyprus, and has dispatched military observers for the supervision of the armistice in the Middle East. Indeed neutral states clearly have a useful part to play in this field, since states involved in warlike disputes prefer peace-keeping troops from neutral countries to those from countries bound by treaties.

It is therefore untrue to say permanent neutrality has lost its meaning. On the contrary neutrality still has a valuable function to perform – precisely because a neutral country's tasks are not confined to securing its own existence and independence but also serve the keeping of peace. A neutral state must never place itself at the disposal of the interests of a single power grouping. By avoiding doing so it will gain for itself the kind of trust and freedom of action hardly ever possessed by a state that is bound by treaties.[15]

Neutrality imposes rights, duties and heavy responsibilities on any country undertaking this obligation, the magnitude of the responsibility emerging particularly strongly at moments of crisis. In many respects, therefore, the policy of a neutral country is more difficult than that of a treaty partner. While a treaty partner is able to consult within its treaty system and is indeed bound by contractual stipulations to do so before taking any major decision, a neutral state has to make up its own mind.

THE QUESTION OF GUARANTEES

The Moscow Memorandum distinguishes between recognition of neutrality and guarantees of the integrity and inviolability of the Austrian state territory by the great powers. Whereas Austria's neutrality has been recognized by most states with which we maintain diplomatic relations, a guarantee of the integrity and inviolability of the territory of the neutral state has not so far been forthcoming. Needless to say, a guarantee goes considerably further than recognition in that it involves an obligation for the guarantor states to intervene if the neutral state's territory is violated by another state.[16] When the 1955 treaty was signed the Austrian government demanded that the four great powers should guarantee the integrity of Austria's territory as envisaged in the Moscow Memorandum; the Soviet Union had declared itself ready to participate in such a guarantee in the second section of the Memorandum. But since the other signatories were not prepared to take such a step no guarantee has so far been given.

We should not make too much of the practical consequences of this situation. After all, the signatories undertook to respect the integrity and inviolability of Austria's territory. If we study the reasons for signing the treaty we find that it served to maintain the international balance of power. Reduced to a simple formula, this means that whereas until 1955 the balance between the great powers was preserved by the quadripartite occupation of Austria, after the signing of the treaty it was preserved by the simultaneous withdrawal of all occupation troops from Austria. Thus the military balance did not change as a result of the treaty. Hence it must still be in the interests of the signatories to maintain this balance by preserving Austria's territory. We will not go far wrong if we assume that the signatory powers are aware of the fact that any unilateral alteration of this balance could not fail to produce a reaction from the other side. It would not therefore be in the interests of the great powers to violate Austria's integrity unilaterally, since the advantages of such a course of action for the signatory or signatories concerned would presumably be outweighed by the disadvantages. This situation – which of course should not be overestimated – provides a certain degree of insurance for Austria, though her security must ultimately and crucially depend on a properly conducted policy of neutrality.

In this connection I made the following declaration in the autumn of 1968:

The treaty concluded in 1955 between the Allied powers and Austria restored Austria's sovereignty and independence. This treaty contains the obligation by the signatories to respect Austria's independence and territorial integrity. Austria has full confidence that the signatories to the treaty are aware of the obligations arising for them from this treaty and will therefore continue in the future to observe Austria's independence and the inviolability of her territory.

I believe that this statement is as valid today as it was then. It will continue to be valid in the future. The simple fact is that the preservation of Austria's integrity is not only in Austria's interest but also in that of the great powers, since its liquidation would inevitably upset the balance of power that has been so labouriously set up in Europe and hence entail unforeseeable consequences in relation to the development of the international situation.

THE ATTITUDE OF THE ORDINARY CITIZEN TO THE NEUTRAL STATE

We have already made the point that permanent neutrality places an obligation on the state alone, not on its citizens. Yet while the individual citizen has no obligations under international law, he does have duties *vis-à-vis* his own country. Professor Verdross refers in this context principally to 'the moral duty of being factual and temperate in the criticism of conditions abroad so as not to complicate our state's foreign policy'.[17] A similar view was expressed during the Second World War by the former Swiss federal councillor Giuseppe Motta:

Neutrality is a concept that concerns only the state. But the citizen has certain duties towards his state. He has, strictly speaking, no such duties towards a foreign country. But he must not cut across the state's neutrality or place himself in opposition to it. This, I believe, is a maxim that any soundly and loyally thinking Swiss will acept without hesitation.[18]

The mass media should therefore strike a balance between an undignified neutrality of opinion on the one hand and intemperate and non-factual criticism on the other.[19] Such a balanced course will be the best and surest support for the government's policy of neutrality which, after all, has only one ultimate aim – the maintenance of the country's independence and integrity.

The signing of the 1955 treaty and the adoption of the constitutional law on permanent neutrality of 26 October 1955 have repeatedly given rise to various interpretations of Austria's neutrality. Although this aspect has already been extensively discussed, it seems appropriate to quote a few major statements by leading Austrian statesmen; these will contribute to a deeper understanding of the Austrian point of view.

During the discussion of the federal constitutional law on Austria's neutrality in the National Assembly, for instance, the federal chancellor, Ing. Julius Raab, stated:

The treaty has provided Austria, for the first time since the foundation of the republic in 1918, with an opportunity for conducting a truly active and constructive foreign policy. For this foreign policy our neutrality will provide a new, promising and lasting foundation. The fact that the present law describes this neutrality as permanent, is of vital importance. Our neutrality is not a temporary, revocable limitation of our sovereignty, something we have reluctantly taken upon ourselves under the pressure of circumstances, but the lasting foundation of a foreign policy which is to ensure peace and prosperity for our country and our people for all time to come.

We are aware that in the field of foreign policy this neutrality imposes a special responsibility upon our country and that it will time and again confront us with difficult decisions. However, we are not afraid of these decisions, for we shall pursue a clear and unambiguous line in our foreign policy, guided by our country's interest and taking account of the European order.

The idea of neutrality has fallen on very fertile soil among the Austrian people. In an astonishingly short period of time this idea, which after all was new to our people, has won universal acceptance. There has also been unanimity on the necessity to defend this neutrality if need be, and hence to raise an army. Naturally there have been some differences of opinion on this point, too, but when raised on a businesslike basis they were rapidly reduced to a common denominator. In an astonishingly short period of time we succeeded in reaching agreement on the organizational form and hence on the

D

preparations for the setting up of the army; these are in full swing and have already made substantial progress. In a commendable manner all four great powers have made available to us stocks of armaments for equipping our new forces.

In his government statement on 17 July 1959 Raab declared:

In my government statement of 1956 I expressed the federal government's conviction that the coming into force of the 1955 treaty and the adoption by the Austrian parliament of the constitutional law on permanent neutrality had heralded a new era of hope and responsibility in Austria's history and politics. I pointed out at the time that neutrality would in future be the guideline of our activities in the field of foreign policy. Nearly four years have passed since then. Time has proved unequivocally that the road we then took on the basis of a free decision has been the right one. Permit me, ladies and gentlemen of this assembly, to declare once more with all solemnity that the new federal government intends to keep in its foreign policy to the clear and unambiguous line prescribed by the federal constitutional law on permanent neutrality. The principles enshrined in it will continue to determine Austria's foreign policy in the future. Similarly, the federal government will scrupulously implement the treaty and the ancillary agreements ensuing from the treaty, such as for instance the Vienna Memorandum.

On 4 May 1960 Dr Bruno Kreisky, then federal minister for foreign affairs, made the following remarks in a lecture to the Economic Society of Zurich:

There are two states in Europe which essentially profess a policy of neutrality—Switzerland and Sweden. Sweden's neutrality, unlike Switzerland's, is not part of the constitution or in any way guaranteed by the great powers. Nor does it represent an obligation undertaken by agreement with one or more countries. What happens is that Sweden endeavours to conduct in peacetime a policy that will make neutrality possible under international law in the event of war. Swedish political terminology therefore prefers to describe her own policy as a policy of freedom from alliances rather than one of neutrality.

If, therefore, Austrian neutrality on the one hand greatly resembles Swiss neutrality in terms of international law, on the other hand the fact that Austria is a member of the United Nations represents a parallel with Sweden's foreign policy. It can therefore be suggested—and I took the liberty of first making this point a few years ago—that between the neutrality of Switzerland and that of Sweden a new Austrian variant of neutrality will evolve in the course of time. The character of our neutrality will have to be determined by ourselves. . . .

In this connection I am anxious to emphasize that the Austrian federal government—as has been repeatedly stated by the Swiss government—has never, from the very outset, allowed any doubt to exist that Austria's neutral position infringes any of the basic rights and freedoms of her citizens. . . .

The policy of neutrality above all involves freedom from military alliances and the obligations arising from them. It does not, however, oblige us to resist the great historical developments in Europe—the neutral states are after all also part of Europe. And they have the right to demand that due account is taken of them in the realization of a European concept.[20]

In his government statement of 2 April 1964 Chancellor Josef Klaus had this to say on Austrian neutrality:

Austria's foreign policy will in future continue to be guided by the principle of permanent neutrality and will respect the obligations arising from it. Its foundation is the federal constitutional law on neutrality of 26 October 1955, which says:
(1) With the object of the lasting maintenance of her independence from without and the inviolability of her territory, Austria declares of her own free will her permanent neutrality. She is resolved to maintain and defend it with all the means at her disposal.
(2) In order to secure these objectives Austria will join no military alliances and will not permit the establishment of military bases of foreign states on her territory.' The text of this law is unambiguous. There is no need for the federal government to provide new interpretations of it. Permanent neutrality entails for Austria the unambiguous obligation of maintaining and defending the independence of our state and the inviolability of its territory with all the means at our disposal.[21]

In his government statement of 20 April 1966 Dr Klaus enlarged on these observations as follows:

Austria's foreign policy must be based on a reliable maxim, beyond the fluctuations of day-to-day politics and party disputes. This basic norm is contained in the federal constitutional law of 26 October 1955, by which Austria has defined her permanent neutrality. The aim springing from this law, an aim that has remained unchanged since, is the lasting maintenance of Austria's independence from outside and the safeguarding of the inviolability of her territory. In striving towards this aim the federal government will continue to be guided by the principle that the interpretation of international obligations ensuing from this federal constitutional law is their own concern alone, while they are fully aware of their parliamentary responsibility to this noble assembly and of the need for observing the generally recognized principles of international law. The federal government will continue to be guided by the principle that international obligations entered into must be strictly respected. They regard endorsement of this principle as the best guarantee of untroubled relations with all states with whom contractual ties exist. I should like to emphasize here in particular that the continuous promotion of friendly and mutually trustful relations with the great powers will continue in the future to form an essential part of our foreign policy.

In conclusion it should be stated once more that Austria's neutrality did not arise from external pressure but was adopted entirely of her own free will. To preserve the integrity of her territory Austria had to keep out of the East–West conflict. The signing of the 1955 treaty was possible only on condition that she kept out of the two military blocs. The adoption of neutral status therefore seemed to the Austrians the most appropriate way of achieving and maintaining the freedom and independence of their country.

In retrospect it can be stated that the decision to adopt permanent neutrality was the right one, since it has brought Austria not only political and economic stability but also international respect such as this small alpine republic had never before enjoyed.

FOREIGN POLICY *VIS-À-VIS* THE FOUR GREAT POWERS

The restoration of Austria's full sovereignty was a vital prerequisite of an independent foreign policy. Since the end of the Second World War Austria's two main parties, the People's Party and the Socialist Party, had jointly supported the country's foreign policy. This co-operation continued in essence even after 1955 and to this day there are no conflicts of principle, though there are of course differences of opinion over methods. Agreement between the two parties was of decisive importance during the struggle for the restoration of Austria's sovereignty and it was this that made a consistent policy of neutrality possible.

After 1955 the most important task in the field of foreign policy was first of all to ensure the enjoyment of the rights and the discharge of the obligations arising from the treaty and from neutral status. It was necessary, for instance, to explain the new point of view arising from self-chosen permanent neutrality both to various government bodies within the country and to the rest of the world. Relations with the signatories to the treaty, i.e. with the four great powers, were and still are of special significance. In a world in which two great power blocs confront each other, the first commandment of a country located right between these two power groupings must be to safeguard its independence in every respect. In the case of a small country such as Austria the degree of its security in this kind of situation is determined by the interest that the great powers have in maintaining its freedom. It follows that the achievement and maintenance of good relations with the signatories to the treaty are a matter of life and death to Austria.

It may be stated that ever since 1955 this interest in maintaining Austria's independence has been present in equal measure in both the great power blocs. Moscow sees the favourable development of its relations with neutral Austria as suitable proof of the truth of its thesis that peaceful coexistence is possible even between states with different social systems. The great western powers – Britain, France and, above all, the United States – have always supported Austria's independence and leave no doubt that this is still their attitude today. If Washington harboured certain misgivings during the final phase of the treaty negotiations, these were due solely to a feeling of anxiety that once the western troops had withdrawn a 'neutralized Austria' might be left unprotected, that she might represent a military vacuum and that – without adequate military forces to maintain her integrity – she might not be in a position to offer resistance. Subsequent developments showed, however, that the situation had been assessed correctly in Vienna. Washington soon came round to the view that in signing the treaty Moscow had taken a genuine, serious step towards a *détente*. Neutral Austria, firmly anchored ideologically in the western world, became a stabilizing factor in this exposed Central European zone – a role she is capable of playing both now and in the future.

As the wish for a *détente* gains ground in East and West, so increasing importance must be attached to Austria's neutrality. As a result, the security of our country is also increasing. It has therefore always been the aim of our foreign policy, and it must continue to be so in the future, to ensure that the great powers' interest in the continued existence of an independent neutral Austria is maintained. In this the policy of neutrality is an important instrument. After all, neutrality is not an end in itself, but a means towards an end – as stressed in the constitutional law on permanent neutrality. The decisive factor – regardless of the great social and economic changes going on round us – has always been Austria's central position in the heart of Europe, in the Danubian region, at the intersection of Latin, Germanic and Slav communities, of the great European routes of communication, and above all near the boundaries of the fields of force of the great power blocs of today. That is why our region, for geographical reasons alone, has an importance in the international interplay of forces that far surpasses the real weight of a small mid-European country.[1] It could easily, thanks to this, become a source of disturbance of the first magnitude, but equally it can become a calming and stabilizing factor beyond the pacification of its own territory, representing an element of tranquillity and safety for its neighbours and indeed for the whole of Europe. Twentieth-century Austria has been the living proof of the effectiveness of this alternative. Thus her leaders bear special responsibility for a great deal more than the primary aim of foreign policy that involves maintaining the security of one's own territory.

History has shown that the acceptance of neutral status, even if guaranteed by the great powers of the day, has not in itself been sufficient to protect the neutral state with any degree of certainty against intervention from outside. Observation of the rules of international law is an ideal demand, which time and again may clash with power interests.

Two elements are decisive for the value or otherwise of neutrality: the readiness of the neutral to defend his independence with all the means at his disposal; and the value attached by the great powers to the preservation of that country's neutral status. To keep alive this interest among other powers is the primary aim of any policy of neutrality that goes beyond purely formal statutory obligations; this is the most important component of any policy of security practised by a small neutral country. It is therefore in Austria's own interest to cultivate interest and confidence in our country's policy of neutrality among the great powers, and especially among the signatories to the 1955 treaty. Such a policy requires a certain measure of restraint, especially on the issues that fall within the immediate areas of tension between the great powers. But it also requires that we should seize every opportunity that could serve its ends and testify to the reliability of our neutral attitude. Such considerations play a part that should not be underrated, especially in Austria's relations with the signatories to the treaty. The primary aim must be, time and again, to strengthen the confidence that these countries feel in Austria's determination consistently and unreservedly to discharge the obligations arising from the treaty and from neutrality.

It is hardly necessary to point out that what has been said

above in no way applies to the ideological sphere. The fact that we belong to the western democratic way of life and that each citizen is entitled to profess the way of life that seems to him the right one remains totally unchallenged and was indeed beyond dispute even when the 1955 treaty was signed. Over the years there has never been anything to indicate the slightest intention on the eastern side to exert any kind of pressure designed to make us take or refrain from taking any action that might have called our basic attitude into question. Indeed I can well imagine that especially for the Soviet Union – which, as I believe, must have had in 1955 an interest in demonstrating by the example of independent and neutral Austria that its concept of peaceful coexistence was realizable – the fact that we belong to the way of thinking of the western world must be a not inconsiderable factor. What both sides expect from Austria is consistency in the stand she has taken, credibility in her day-to-day policies and the avoidance of any temptation to allow herself to be harnessed to the interests of power politics on either side.

This account cannot go in detail into all aspects of Austria's relations with the signatories to the treaty since it was signed in 1955. But we can state without exaggeration that Austria's relaions with all four powers have developed favourably. Washington appreciates the fact that we have not forgotten the support that the United States gave us during the difficult postwar years. It appears that we are one of the few countries to recall this help with gratitude. We are linked to London by bonds of traditional friendship, which have been further strengthened by our joint membership of Efta. Relations with France have also developed in an entirely amicable way and the realization has been gaining ground on both sides that these relations are certainly capable of further development; whereas our traditionally close ties in the cultural field have been most gratifyingly intensified since the Second World War, the possibilities for economic co-operation have not yet been fully exhausted. It is to be expected that the mixed commission set up in connection with the French premier's visit to Vienna in 1967 will remedy matters.

Austria's relations with the Soviet Union have acquired a special importance through the signing of the 1955 treaty and the part played by Moscow in this. To attempt to spotlight the decisive role played throughout Austrian history by our country's relations with Russia would go beyond the scope of this book. Developments since the Second World War have further increased their importance. New and amicable foundations for Austro-Soviet relations were undoubtedly laid in 1955.

The motives that induced the Soviet Union to agree to sign the treaty have been discussed in connection with the events that led to this step. We now know that there was disagreement among the ranks of the Soviet leadership on how to proceed on the Austrian issue. The signing of the Austrian treaty inaugurated the new Soviet line of coexistence and it was intended, among other things, to testify to the sincerity of the Soviet leadership in its policy of peaceful co-operation among all states regardless of their ideological or political systems. Thus the signing of the treaty and the establishment of Austria's permanent neutrality are seen by Moscow as a success for Soviet foreign policy.

The treaty and the obligation of permanent neutrality were designed to safeguard Austria's independence from Germany beyond question. Article 4 of the treaty, like the phrase 'neutrality on the Swiss model' in the Moscow Memorandum, clearly represents to the Soviet Union an adequate legal guarantee against a renewed *Anschluss* of Austria to Germany. In many conversations with Soviet statesmen I have repeatedly observed the deep-seated anxiety they feel about a renewed penetration of West German influence into Austria. Moscow evidently fears that the Federal Republic's growing influence on Austria's economy might inevitably lead to an intensification of her political influence and ultimately to a renewed absorption of Austria. It certainly seems that the treaty and the law of neutrality are regarded by the Soviet Union as an important barrier against tendencies of this kind.

Since the signing of the treaty and the adoption of the Austrian constitutional law on permanent neutrality there has been no serious strain on amicable relations, not even under such difficult external conditions as during the Hungarian rising or the Czechoslovak crisis. The relationship of trust between Vienna and Moscow has been further strengthened by a number of official visits. Major differences of opinion do admittedly exist on the question of the regulation of our relations with the European Economic Community; from the Soviet point of view this is not so much a problem of economics or international law as a political problem. These considerations are clearly also coloured by misgivings about Austria's economic infiltration by the Federal Republic of Germany, the most powerful partner in the European Economic Community; these are the kind of considerations that we have discussed under the heading of possible political consequences.

AUSTRIA AND HER NEIGHBOURS

Considerations of security also lie at the heart of Austrian policy with regard to her neighbours. The more peaceful the situation on Austria's frontiers, the less the friction in her relations with her immediate neighbours, the greater will be her safety. Nearly half her territory borders on countries of the eastern bloc. That is why ever since the rebirth of the Second Republic, and more particularly since the signing of the 1955 treaty, the reduction of what were initially considerable tensions along her eastern frontiers and the normalization of her relations with her neighbour countries along those frontiers have been seen as one of the primary tasks of Austrian policy. This task was fulfilled in a pragmatic manner, and an attempt was made to clear up such problems as the unsolved question of property, and to establish human contacts in both directions. We must not forget that for several centuries these nations belonged to a common empire, as a result of which a large number of personal, family and other relationships have come into being across today's frontiers. We are therefore developing our co-operation with these states in the economic, technological, scientific and cultural spheres, and in this way are making our contribution to peaceful development in the region.

We are linked with our western neighbours by a common ideology and way of life, and with Switzerland also by the status of permanent neutrality. Relations with the Federal Republic of Germany have been unclouded by any traumas since the difficult property problem was settled – in contrast to the prewar situation. Our relations with Italy were until recently coloured by the unsolved issue of South Tyrol. After many years of effort it finally proved possible towards the end of 1969 to reach an agreement with Italy which has created the prerequisites for a satisfactory settlement of this problem.

8

AUSTRIA AND EUROPEAN INTEGRATION

The idea of European integration is deeply rooted in Austrian thinking. The multinational state of the Austro-Hungarian monarchy may have played a part in making a striving towards more intensive co-operation between European nations more visible in Austria than in other countries. The collapse of the monarchy and the emergence of the small alpine republic, far from weakening such efforts, tended to strengthen them – not least for economic reasons, since the First Republic lacked any kind of hinterland, which would have been necessary for economic consolidation. It was therefore not surprising that leanings towards European integration received new impetus, and it was an Austrian, Count Richard Coudenhove-Kalergi, who started the Pan-European Movement after the collapse of the old monarchy.

The restoration of the republic in 1945 occurred under more favourable conditions than the foundation of the First Republic, in spite of the painful effects of the Second World War. The occupying powers realized that Austria had to be helped, particularly in the economic sphere, if she was to survive in the long term as an independent state. But Austria was only one aspect of the great European problem of the postwar years, when our continent was in danger of breaking up from the consequences of the war. Famine and destitution were not confined to the defeated countries but were more or less universal throughout Europe. It was against this background that the Paris conference of sixteen West-European countries was held from 12 July to 22 September 1947 and that it worked out a European reconstruction programme as the basis for Marshall Plan aid. On 16 April 1948 Austria, in common with fifteen countries in Western Europe, signed the convention concerning the Organization for European Economic Co-operation (OEEC). This convention may be seen as the foundation stone of a whole series of further efforts aimed at closer economic co-operation between the countries of Europe.

THE ESTABLISHMENT OF EFTA

Perhaps the most important step in this direction was the setting up of the European Coal and Steel Community on 18 April 1951, and the signing of the Treaty of Rome on the establishment of the European Economic Community and of Euratom on 25 March 1957. These decisions represented the nucleus of European economic integration but at the same time placed the European countries outside the community in a difficult position. The barriers erected round the EEC resulted in discrimination against exports from other European states, with the result that the latter were faced with the need to take steps to safeguard their foreign trade. The result was the foundation of the European Free Trade Area (Efta). Its members were Britain, Sweden, Norway, Denmark, Austria, Switzerland, Portugal and subsequently, as an associate member, Finland – i.e. the countries that maintained closest economic links with the EEC area but were suffering most from the division of Europe by customs and trade barriers.

Yet within a year of its being set up a feeling began to gain ground within Efta that this association had not fulfilled one of its main tasks – to remove, by an arrangement with the Six, the economic disadvantages suffered by the Efta countries. These reflections were also made in Austrian government circles, but there was a sufficiently realistic attitude in Vienna for it to be recognized that such bridge-building presupposed a corresponding political will on the part of the EEC.

Britain clearly did not doubt the existence of such a readiness on the part of the EEC countries and on 9 August 1961 she officially applied to the EEC to open negotiations to examine the possibility of her admission. Thus the earlier view held by the Efta states, that the rift between them and the EEC should be bridged by a multilateral solution, had been abandoned.

This step had of course been preceded by consultations between the Efta governments, as for instance at the Efta Council of Ministers meeting in London on 27 and 28 June, and in Geneva on 28 July. At the first meeting a declaration was issued to the effect that Efta would be kept in being at least until satisfactory solutions had been worked out in negotiations, taking into account the legitimate interests of all its member states, to enable all of them to participate in an integrated European market from the same moment. The declaration further stated that a solution that was confined to only a few of the Efta countries could not under any circumstances be regarded as satisfactory.

The Austrian federal government, drawing its conclusions from a totally altered situation following Britain's application for EEC membership, announced on 31 July that Austria too was prepared to enter into negotiations concerning participation in an all-European market, that in so doing she would strive for economic arrangements, taking into account in particular the interests of her trade policy, and that she would enter into only such obligations as were in line with her international status.[1]

Proceeding from this foreign policy stand and in view of the fact that not only Britain but also Denmark had meanwhile applied for admission to the EEC, and that Norway was considering such an application, Austria intensified her contacts with the remaining neutral Efta countries – Switzerland and Sweden. During September 1961 talks were held at an official level in Vienna between the three neutrals; their conclusions were on the agenda of a ministerial conference of neutral Efta states held on 19 October, again in Vienna. The ministers – Friedrich Wahlen and Hans Schaffner (for Switzerland), Gunnar Lange and Gösta Netzen (for Sweden) and Dr Bruno Kreisky and Dr Fritz Bock (for Austria)–arrived at the unanimous view that neutrality was no obstacle to participation in Europe's economic integration through association in a suitable form.

At an Efta ministerial conference held in Geneva on 20 and 21 November Austria, Sweden and Switzerland informed their Efta partners of this view and of their intention to propose some form of association in approximately identical notes to the EEC.

While Austria was thus preparing for bilateral steps to solve her economic relations with the Common Market, the Soviet ambassador in Austria, Viktor Avilov, had presented a note to the federal chancellor on 27 August 1961 in which Austria was requested to give the Soviet government an explanation of her intention of entering into negotiations concerning participation in the Common Market. On 2 October 1961 Dr Gorbach had handed Avilov the note of reply decided upon by the federal government. This stated that Austria was interested in maintaining the best possible economic relations with all countries regardless of their political regimes. For this reason Austria could not remain inactive in the face of certain economic developments in Europe, and this was why a unanimous resolution by the Austrian parliament on 21 June 1961 had emphasized Austria's special interest in the economic integration of Europe. The Austrian government had approved the Efta declaration of 31 July 1961 and had re-emphasized in a statement that Austria would attempt to achieve within the framework of European economic integration only such economic arrangements as would take into account the particular interests of her trade policy and would enter only into such obligations as were in line with her international status. It was on these lines that consultations were taking place with the other neutral Efta states. As soon as the Austrian federal government had arrived at any final decisions concerning Austria's participation in the economic integration of Europe, they would not fail to notify all the countries with whom Austria maintained intensive economic relations of their intentions.[2]

A week after this reply to the Soviet Union the committee for questions of integration set up by the government met under the chairmanship of the federal chancellor to discuss the problems that might arise as a result of European economic integration and, more particularly, of Austria's association with the EEC.

In order to explain Austria's attitude to the problem of integration to the United States of America as well, the trade minister, Dr Bock, travelled on 23–4 October to Washington, where he met the US secretary for trade, Luther Hodges, and the under-secretary of state, George Ball.

At the beginning of December the budget debate in the Austrian National Assembly finally provided an opportunity both for the deputies and for the federal government to hold a detailed discussion of Austria's future position in the economic integration of Europe. The various speakers were unanimous that Austria regarded her permanent neutrality as unassailable and that she would ensure that this neutrality emerged undiminished from her negotiations with the EEC.

AUSTRIA'S EFFORTS FOR EEC ASSOCIATION

Bolstered by this view within the National Assembly, the Austrian government approved on 12 December 1961 the wording of a letter[3] in which Austria proposed to the EEC the opening of negotiations with a view to coming to an exclusively economic arrangement that would take account of Austria's permanent neutrality and international agreements and would enable her to discharge at any time the obligations arising from them.

On the same day the Soviet ambassador delivered to the Austrian government another *aide-mémoire* in which the view was expressed that Austria's association with the EEC was incompatible with her status of permanent neutrality and the obligations arising from the 1955 treaty. But the letter approved by the federal government, signed by Dr Kreisky and addressed to the president of the EEC Council, Professor Ludwig Erhard, was already on its way to Brussels and it was presented to the secretary-general of the EEC Council of Ministers, Christian Calmes, by the Austrian ambassador to the European communities, Dr Ernst Lemberger, on 15 December.

After receiving the head of the Austrian mission Calmes also received the Swedish and Swiss ambassadors and accepted letters from the Swedish foreign minister, Östen Lunden, and from the president of the Swiss Political Department, F. T. Wahlen, in which Sweden and Switzerland requested the opening of negotiations that would enable them to contribute to the establishment of an integrated European market.[4]

Needless to say, all the participating governments had realized from the outset that a solution for the neutral countries could be found only if the negotiations with Britain that had been opened in Brussels in the early autumn of 1961 and had in the meantime been conducted in considerable detail – at times with an astonishing eye for detail – reached a successful conclusion. Patience was therefore called for and it was hardly surprising that Austria was not invited to Brussels by the EEC Council of Ministers for a rather more detailed exposition of her ideas until six months after the submission of her application.

The exposition was given to the foreign ministers of the EEC countries by Dr Bruno Kreisky, the federal minister for foreign affairs, in the presence of Dr Fritz Bock, federal minister for trade and reconstruction, on 28 July 1962.[5] Having clarified Austria's position and aims, he pointed out that as a continuation of the unremitting interest shown by her since the end of the Second World War in European economic integration, she was now hoping for an arrangement that would enable her to participate in such integration and would at the same time take her political status into account.

The Swedes explained their point of view on the same day as the Austrians; the Swiss followed on 24 September 1962. All three declarations had been worked out in close collaboration between Vienna, Berne and Stockholm.

While the technical preliminaries for the impending preparatory talks between Austria and the EEC were being set in motion in Vienna and Brussels, it became increasingly obvious in the autumn of 1962 that so far, despite all the optimistic statements being made by the participants, the negotiations between the Common Market and Britain had not by any means reached the political heart of the matter. When these negotiations eventually foundered, or rather were postponed indefinitely, as a result of France's veto on 29 January 1963, this was registered in Austria as a highly regrettable but by no means unexpected event.

At any rate, the applications by Britain, Denmark and Norway for membership were no longer topical. And although Sweden and Switzerland upheld their applications for association with the EEC, they did not expect an early resumption of the relevant negotiations. In Austria, on the other hand, the view was gaining ground that the collapse of Britain's negotiations was no reason why Austria's efforts to come to an agreement should be similarly shelved for an indefinite period. Instead, Austria's special situation and her specific economic conditions induced the federal government to notify the six EEC countries on 26 February that she was still interested in the application she had handed in on 15 December being discussed by the Community. At the same time an *aide-mémoire* was presented, urging the setting of a date for exploratory talks between Austria and the Community.

Now that they were spared from negotiations with Britain, the EEC Council of Ministers found the time to take up the Austrian issue once again and on 2 April instructed the Commission to work out within four weeks a feasibility study of the problems raised by future economic relations between Austria and the Community.

By coincidence, the day after the Council of Ministers' decision the newly formed Austrian federal government under Dr Gorbach emphasized in a government statement in the National Assembly on the integration problem,

... that Austria declares herself in favour of absolute loyalty to treaties and to the strict observance of her freely declared neutrality. The most pressing question in the field of foreign policy will be the regulation of Austria's relations with the European Economic Community. It is a matter of course that only such an arrangement would be considered as took account of the maintenance of Austria's permanent neutrality and her international obligations.[6]

After some delay, towards the end of May 1963, the EEC Commission submitted the report on Austria demanded by the Council of Ministers; this listed the various possible solutions for an agreement. On the basis of this report the Council of Ministers authorized the Commission on 31 May of the same year to conduct the necessary talks with the Austrian mission in Brussels.

This represented the first step. True, these were at first only what were known as exploratory talks; but it was reasonable to assume that, since they were not of their nature binding on either side, they would cover all the fundamental questions in the fullest detail.

Thus as early as 10 June the Austrian Council of Ministers approved the necessary instructions to their ambassador, Ernst Lemberger, who was authorized to resume the talks on the lines agreed upon and with the collaboration of representatives from the specialized departments concerned.

These principles ran essentially as follows:

– the observance of the obligations resulting from the Austrian state treaty;

– the preservation of legal obligations and foreign policy interests arising from Austria's status as a permanently neutral state;

– a far-reaching acceptance of the common agricultural policy arising from the Treaty of Rome; the total abolition of customs and of the surviving quota restrictions on imports between Austria and the EEC within a period to be negotiated;

– Austria's readiness to accept the customs level of the EEC tariff, with the proviso that possible exceptions might have to be negotiated;

– Austria's readiness to follow future customs fluctuations of the EEC external tariff autonomously as far as possible;

– Austria must however reserve the right to be allowed to sign customs and other trade treaties with third countries on her own behalf, in which case her participation in the European Free Trade zone must be taken into consideration;

– Austria's readiness to co-ordinate other spheres of her economic policy with the Six.[7]

On 3 May 1963 the Soviet ambassador again called on Dr Gorbach and handed him another *aide-mémoire* defining his government's attitude to the new Austrian cabinet's statement of 3 April. Among other things, this stated that 'Austria's accession to the EEC in one form or another' conflicted with neutrality and with the 1955 treaty.

The first round of preparatory talks at expert level was held in Brussels from 4 to 9 July and consisted primarily of listing the questions that were to be solved. The talks next concentrated on customs matters, including the effects on trade policy, the general situation of agriculture, institutional questions and Austria's membership of Efta – the latter being raised by the EEC. When the exploratory talks were continued – with interruptions they went on until December 1963 – the subjects under discussion were: the effects of permanent neutrality and the treaty of 15 May 1955 on the hoped-for arrangement; the adaptation of the Austrian customs tariff to the EEC external tariff; transport policy; movements of capital; rules of competition; questions concerning the right of registration of companies; services and institutional matters. Neutrality as such was not discussed, since both delegations proceeded from the implicit view that interpretation of the obligations arising from neutrality was a matter for Austria alone.

The question raised by the EEC concerning Austria's continued membership of Efta after she had come to an arrangement with the EEC led to a lively discussion among the Austrian people while the exploratory talks were still in progress. This discussion was based on an incorrect piece of information which stated that the Austrian delegation of experts had agreed that Austria would leave Efta. In fact Austria took the view in Brussels that the discontinuation of her Efta membership, which the EEC wanted, could not begin to be discussed until agreement and clarity had been reached between the two delegations on the essential principles of the association agreement. At this stage of purely preparatory and exploratory talks the Austrian side was clearly in no position to take a stand on the issue of dual membership – a solution that Austria had always preferred.

After the conclusion of the exploratory phase of these contacts the EEC Commission expressly stated that they were in a position to prepare a comprehensive report for the EEC Council of Ministers. But it was no less than five months before the results of these exploratory talks were summarized and it was not until 3 June 1964 that the report recommending the opening of official negotiations with Austria was submitted to the Council of Ministers. On 30 July the Council took note of it and instructed the committee of permanent representatives to work out a draft brief for negotiations.

The permanent representatives reported to the Council of Ministers on their discussions on a number of occasions and on each of these the Council expressed its hope that work on the Austrian issue would be expedited. But in Austria the impression was gaining ground that matters were hanging fire in Brussels. Although the federal government realized that the lengthy talks with the EEC had clarified a number of questions, they nevertheless felt inclined, on 24 November, to authorize the minister for state and reconstruction to have notes presented to the governments of EEC member states by the various Austrian ambassadors. These notes requested that, in view of the basic concepts set out in the exploratory talks and the urgency of an early settlement of Austria's relations with the EEC, an early start to the official negotiations should be approved.

Largely as a result of this Austrian initiative the EEC Council Ministers discussed Austria at length on 30 November 1964, together with the report submitted by the permanent representatives on an agreement with Austria. It was found that all the ministers were basically in favour of the opening of negotiations as urged by Austria, but that opinions were still divided on the nature of the agreement. Thus Italy – in line with its doctrine of association formulated in May of that year – merely favoured a preferential trade treaty, while the other member states inclined towards a solution in line with Article XXIV of Gatt.

The decision eventually taken by the Council at this meeting stated – by way of reconciling the differences revealed – that the question of relations between Austria and the EEC could not be settled by a classical trade agreement which merely contained non-discriminatory provisions. The committee of permanent representatives was therefore instructed by the Council to investigate, as a matter of priority, the feasibility of a solution under Article XXIV of Gatt and to examine an alternative solution based on a special Gatt regulation (Article XXV: 'Waiver').

When the EEC Council of Ministers again discussed Austria on 2 February 1965 there was still no draft brief that all the member states could have endorsed. But there was a mounting feeling within the EEC Council of Ministers – as the chairman, the French foreign minister, Couve de Murville, put it – that there was no longer any excuse for delaying the opening of negotiations with Austria any further. So the Council instructed the permanent representatives to work out a draft of a first brief for the Council's session of 2 March to enable negotiations with Austria to be opened within the shortest possible time.

It was largely due to Jean Rey, the commissioner for external relations of the EEC Commission, that this obligation was adopted, and that a month later, on 2 March, the Council did unanimously approve a brief authorizing the Commission to open a first phase of negotiations with Austria.

It was the Council's intention that these negotiations with Austria should start at once, and that they should first of all discover whether agreement was possible on the basis laid down in the brief. The principal points at issue were: removal of trade obstacles between Austria and the Community; future arrangements in the sphere of Austrian external tariffs and the external tariffs of the Community, in particular Austria's customs regulations *vis-à-vis* third countries; the need to harmonize economic policies on both sides.

Negotiations between Austria and the EEC were opened in Brussels on 19 March. The leader of the Austrian delegation, Dr Bock, in the presence of Dr Kreisky made a statement repeating the principles that had guided Austria's representatives during the exploratory talks; these would continue to be the Austrian delegation's guidelines during the impending negotiations. Austria hoped for an agreement covering the following areas:

– The removal of customs and of any remaining quota restrictions between Austria and the EEC within a period to be agreed by negotiation;

– Austria's willingness to adjust her present customs level to the EEC tariff (possible exceptions to be the subject of negotiations) and to follow any future customs movements of the EEC external tariff as far as possible in an autonomous manner;

– a far-reaching adjustment of Austrian agricultural policy to the common agricultural policy arising from the Treaty of Rome;

– Austria's willingness to co-ordinate to a considerable extent others areas of her economic policy in so far as this was necessary for the avoidance of competitive distortions;

– Austria's reservation of the right to make customs and other trade agreements with third countries in her own name.

On the customs problem the Austrian minister for trade added that the reduction of Austrian customs *vis-à-vis* the EEC should be effected within a period of about four or five years. He hoped that the EEC member countries would be prepared for their part to apply the EEC internal customs tariffs to imports from the start of the agreement.

Repeating parts of the declaration of 28 July 1962, Dr Bock observed:

The state treaty and neutrality thus represent the foundations of Austria's sovereignty and independence, and that is why the Austrian federal government, in its letter of 15 December 1961, declared that it wished to enter into an economic agreement with the European Economic Community that would allow for the maintenance of permanent neutrality as well as Austria's international agreements and enable her at all times to discharge the obligations arising from these.

These international obligations, he continued, entailed certain consequences that Austria would have to allow for in the coming negotiations. These included the proviso that in the event of an imminent or existing armed conflict, the application of certain stipulations of the agreement, or possibly the entire agreement, might have to be temporarily suspended. Similarly, the right of termination must be provided for since a permanently neutral state could not sign any such agreement without the right of termination. In certain circumstances, moreover, participation in acts of economic policy directed against third countries might have to be refused even in peacetime, whenever such actions served exclusively political ends.[8]

The first round of talks was held from 22 to 29 April 1965. On the agenda were the prerequisites for the establishment of a free exchange of goods between Austria and the Community in the industrial and manufacturing sector, in particular the removal of obstacles to trade as well as bringing the Austrian customs tariff into line with that of the Community, and problems connected with this. The second round of negotiations (17–21 May) was concerned with agriculture, as was the third round (21–5 June), but at the latter trade with the East and the external tariff were also discussed. The bringing into line of economic policies was covered in the fourth round (28 September to 1 October) and in the fifth (6 –10 December). Finally the question of institutions was examined between 31 January and 4 February 1966. This exhausted the Commission's negotiating brief. If negotiations with Austria were to be continued a new brief would be needed.

In order to work out such a new brief, or rather to speed it up, the Commission submitted its report on the first three rounds of negotiations to the EEC Council of Ministers as early as 21 October 1965. The proceedings of the fourth, fifth and sixth rounds were summed up in a paper submitted to the Council on 27 April 1966. The sub-committee for Austria of the permanent representatives of the member states in Brussels examined the two reports during the next few months. So did the permanent representatives, and on 25 July and 26 October they informed the Council of Ministers on the state of their consultations. Although on each of these occasions the Council of Ministers expressed the hope that it would, within the near future, be able to concern itself with the draft of a second, supplementary, brief, the discussion of the reports within the EEC made slow progress.

Even during the exploratory talks the Italian view – briefly mentioned above, to the effect that highly industrialized European countries should not associate with the Community but should merely regulate their relations with it by way of a trade agreement – had had a delaying effect on the talks. But now misgivings were being voiced on the French side as well; it was becoming increasingly clear that the special agreement hoped for by Austria after the collapse of the British application had not by any means received the basic political approval of all member states, despite the *rapprochement* reached on practical matters.

This may have been due to a variety of causes. One of them was what became known as the EEC 'crisis', which had broken out on 30 June 1965 as a result of differences of opinion among the member states on the financing of the common agricultural policy and which was not cleared up until 17 and 18 January 1966, in Luxemburg, when the French representatives returned to the EEC Council. This crisis resulted in the alignment of France against the other five EEC members on substantial issues concerning the future development of the Community and temporarily led to a degree of paralysis in the Community's various bodies, both internally and in foreign relations. This was bound to affect the Austrian issue, which France, in particular, feared might establish a dangerous precedent. Moreover, just as the negotiating delegations of Austria and the Community had moved closer together over some far from unimportant areas of the future agreement, France seemed increasingly to want to call the political desirability of any form of agreement with Austria into question – a political desirability tested against the basic line of French foreign policy as developed by the then president of the French Republic.

Against this background the visit paid to Austria by the Soviet head of state, N. V. Podgorny, from 14 to 21 November 1966 was of particular significance. President Podgorny took the opportunity to state that in the Soviet view Austria could not enter into anything other than a trade agreement with the member states of the European Economic Community and that any comprehensive agreement would run counter to her international position.

THE NEGOTIATIONS CONTINUE

A fortnight later, on 6 and 7 December 1966, the EEC Council of Ministers approved a second partial brief for the resumption of negotiations, defining the Community's position on the regulation of trade in manufactured goods, on agriculture and on Austria's trade with Eastern Europe. France voted in favour of the brief, along with the rest of the EEC members, but Couve de Murville made his agreement subject to the condition that before the negotiations with Austria were concluded a fundamental discussion should be held among EEC members on whether a special comprehensive agreement with Austria was desirable from the Community's point of view, and whether, considering the general situation in Europe, it would be free from political risk.

Thus negotiations between Austria and the Community continued. In the seventh round of talks, from 13 to 16 December, the two delegations dealt with manufacturing industries and with trade with the East. The eighth round, from 30 January to 2 February 1967, was mainly concerned with agricultural questions. At this point the Commission had once again reached the limits of its second partial brief, which meant that after a period of two years negotiations were concluded for the time being.

Six weeks later the Commission submitted to the Council its report on the seventh and eighth rounds of talks and on the conclusions it had drawn from them. A partial report on agriculture was supplied later, in early May.

With regard to the mechanics of the negotiations it should be pointed out that the possible content of the future agreement had been subjected to a dual reading, in the course of which the two negotiating delegations achieved considerable *rapprochement* on a number of important points. Agreement was reached in particular on the following:

– the total removal of customs and other obstacles to trade

between Austria and the EEC within four years and without
any exceptions;
– the bringing into line of the Austrian customs tariff with
the communal customs tariff of the EEC;
– Austria was to be entitled to negotiate and conclude on her
own behalf customs and trade agreements with third countries
and in particular to regulate in an autonomous manner her
trade relations with the eastern states;
– the EEC delegation also acknowledged the neutrality
reservations demanded by Austria and declared its agreement
to a termination and suspension clause.

It did not prove difficult to reach agreement on a body in
which Austria and the EEC would be represented by an equal
number of votes, so that neither party to the agreement could be
outvoted on the implementation or administration of the agreement. In addition an arbitration body was to be set up, but the
details of this were left open.

Of course a number of important questions had not yet been
clarified:
– the question, for instance, of the pace at which customs
tariffs were to be abolished within four years;
– the extent to which agriculture was to be included in the
free traffic – there was agreement on the principle but not on
the date;
– on the issue of trade with the East, the question of whether
Austria could resort to her special and autonomous measures
for the benefit of her eastern trade relations preventively, i.e.
before a recession of eastern trade had taken place, or
correctively, i.e. after the event.

This list shows that the negotiations conducted between 1955
and 1967 had yielded some decisive advantages and that there
were no insuperable difficulties on factual questions.[9] But matters
were totally different in the general political sphere. The fundamental reservation raised by Couve de Murville when the second
partial brief was adopted had been a clear sign that the continuation of negotiations – let alone their conclusion–was by no
means imminent.

The federal government were fully aware of this, which was
why, in spite of the *rapprochement* achieved in the negotiations
so far and the entirely favourable conclusions in the Commis-

sion's report on the last phase of negotiations, they addressed an *aide-mémoire* to the EEC governments and the Commission at the beginning of May 1967. In this they summed up once more the Austrian stand in the negotiations and defined her wishes, both in the economic sphere and on the question of neutrality. The Austrian minister of trade presented this document to the French foreign minister personally on 12 May.

The EEC Council of Ministers in fact instructed the permanent representatives on 5 June 1967 to report as soon as possible on the state of negotiations with Austria, and in doing so to take account of all available documents concerning the subject, including in particular Austria's most recent *aide-mémoire*. This decision was chiefly due to the Belgian foreign minister, Pierre Harmel, who had urged the speediest possible approval of a final brief – if possible by the end of July 1967. His intervention in favour of speeding up the procedure on Austria had been triggered off by a promise made by his premier, Paul van den Boeynants, during an official visit to Austria from 25 to 27 May in that year. It was therefore to be expected that at its next meeting, on 10 July, the Council of Ministers would seriously examine the comprehensive paper on the state of negotiations with Austria prepared, in accordance with its instructions, by the permanent representatives and that it would consider the final approval of a third and last brief for the conclusion of the negotiations.

But this was not to be. Just as the permanent representatives were engaged on the preparatory work for the Council meeting Austria was removed from the agenda on 28 June. Italy's permanent representative at the EEC, Giorgio Bombassei, had declared himself unable, in the absence of instructions, to contribute to a useful discussion of the Austrian problem. At first this appeared to be nothing more than one of those familiar procedural difficulties to which the negotiating partners of the Six had become accustomed over the years. But within twenty-four hours, on 29 June, the issue took on a new dimension.

On that day, at a consultative meeting of heads of delegations concerned with the special ministerial council of the European Coal and Steel Community, the Italian secretary of state, Franco Malfatti, read out a statement to the effect that the Austrian application for an agreement with the EEC would be opposed by

Italy at all levels until she was convinced, in connection with the South Tyrol problem, that Austrian territory was not being used for organizing terrorist activities on Italian soil or as a refuge for terrorists. The special ministerial council of the European Coal and Steel Community thereupon abandoned its intention of examining Austria's application, first lodged on 15 December 1965, for the opening of negotiations to regulate her relations with the European Coal and Steel Community.

At the meeting of the permanent representatives in Brussels on 30 June 1967 Bombassei made an identical statement to that of Malfatti. Thus the Italian veto was complete.

Of course the Austrian government notified the member states of the European Community that it considered Italy's attempt to link the South Tyrol problem with Austria's efforts to regulate her economic relations with the EEC and the ECSC to be quite unjustified. But the prospects for the Austrian negotiations being continued or concluded on the same basis as before were now virtually nil.

No support was to be expected from the remaining EEC members at this time. They could not and did not wish to interfere in the dispute that had arisen between Austria and Italy and hoped that this could be settled by bilateral negotiations between those concerned. The Italian veto also relieved the French government of the obligation to implement the reservation made on the Austrian negotiations by Couve de Murville and to demand a thorough-going debate on the political desirability of the special agreement aspired to by Austria.

It is therefore an open question whether sooner or later the Austrian negotiations might not have ground to a halt for other reasons, even without the Italian veto. This became particularly clear during the state visit to Vienna of the French premier, Georges Pompidou, and Couve de Murville, from 13 to 16 September 1967. What Austrian diplomats had until then only suspected was now confirmed in the talks between the Austrian federal chancellor and his French opposite number. France regarded Austria's wish for a comprehensive settlement of her economic relations with the Common Market as part of the wider problem of the enlargement of the EEC, and not therefore as one that could be solved in isolation. Thus for the first time a standpoint was clearly adopted that was to determine France's attitude to the Austrian government's efforts at integration over the next few years.

The crystallization of the French attitude during 1967 was undoubtedly connected with the fact that Britain,[10] Ireland, Denmark and Norway had meanwhile submitted new applications for admission. The question of priority for the EEC's internal development over any extension – in the French view an issue that touched the very foundations of the Community's existence – had thus once again become acute. To Austria, in view of her special position and her economic interests, the prospect of being closely linked from now on with the problem of the general widening of the EEC was unsatisfactory. Besides, what Austria had long foreseen now occurred – the exchange of goods with the Efta countries, which had removed all their customs barriers in the field of manufactured goods on 1 January 1967 (sooner than planned), was growing vigorously, while there was a simultaneous decline in Austria's exports to the Common Market. This decline was in fact an absolute one, in view of the slump within the EEC. Austria's imports from the EEC, on the other hand, continued to rise.

It was no consolation that this development was affecting not only Austria but all the other countries that were outside the Community and were interested in entering into agreements with it.

Towards the end of 1967 the fact had to be faced that Austria's efforts and her concept of an economic agreement with the EEC had been wrecked by factors over which she had no control, or only very slight control. The widening of the EEC through the admission of new members seemed to have no prospect of realization (considering that France had again vetoed Britain's admission on 18–19 December 1967) and the creation of a large European market by way of special arrangements with countries that were prevented from becoming members did not seem a possibility either. The European constellation was clearly not yet ripe for major solutions.

Austria's integration policy was therefore in a blind alley when I took over the foreign ministry on 19 January 1968. There could be no question of simply resuming the negotiations that had been conducted by Austria and the EEC from March 1965 onwards and which, for reasons largely beyond Austria's control, had been at a standstill since February 1967. Any efforts along these lines would have been unrealistic so long as the problem of South Tyrol and the question of a global extension of the EEC, with which Austria's hopes of a separate agreement were in effect being linked, remained unsolved.

The appropriate Austrian circles therefore turned their attention first to a task which – without prejudice to the grand objective – held greater prospect of success at that time. This involved obtaining as soon as possible, by way of concrete separate negotiations with the EEC, such trade relief for Austria's manufacturing industry as was needed to maintain her traditional relations with the Common Market economies. Such negotiations were subsequently conducted and quite considerable advantages were gained for various Austrian exports to the Community, especially in the agricultural sector. The overall complex of these separate methods of relief was the subject of talks between an Austrian delegation and representatives of the Commission in Brussels on 18 and 19 July 1968.

At the same time the federal government continued, with interest unabated, to watch the discussions that had been proceeding within the European communities since the beginning of the year. These were designed to keep the issue of the enlargement of the EEC on the agenda in some form or other and to find solutions to halt the stagnation in the process of integration. The government's attention was focused mainly on the trade policy arrangements proposed in the joint Franco-German communiqué of 15 February 1968 during the visit of the German foreign minister, Willy Brandt, to Paris. These were intended to bring about the creation of a European preferential zone and to represent an interim solution designed to facilitate the subsequent enlargement of the Community, without being a substitute for membership. This preferential zone was to be open to the Community, to the candidates for admission and to the European states that had applied for association with the Community or for some similar arrangement.

It soon emerged, however, that the two proponents, France and the Federal Republic of Germany, did not have quite the same ideas about the precise meaning of the proposal or the identity of the participants. The main feature would have been a partial, stage-by-stage reduction of customs for industrial manufactured goods between the participants in these arrangements. In the agricultural sector a settlement appropriate to the advantage granted in the industrial sector was to be conceded, in the form of mutual preference for as many products as possible. On this point France had more concrete ideas than Germany and allowed it to be understood that in the agricultural sector she expected collaterals in favour of the Community at a price level between that of the world market and EEC prices. European agricultural exporters were to receive preferential treatment on EEC markets. France accepted the German view that these trade arrangements would have to be compatible with Gatt stipulations but rejected any specific mention of Article XXIV of Gatt.

Austria welcomed these ideas and as early as March 1968 instructed her ambassadors to the six member states and to the Commission of the European communities to express her interest in participating in talks or negotiations on these proposals. At the beginning of July the government repeated their initiative and urgently requested the governments of the EEC member states and the Commission to meet her request and ensure that she could participate from the outset in all negotiations on these arrangements.

The United Nations General Assembly in the spring of 1968 provided me with an opportunity for a talk with the French foreign minister, Michel Debré. During this I gained the impression that Debré was not opposed to a simple preferential trade arrangement on the basis of linear customs restrictions between Austria and the Community.

The question of a preferential trade arrangement of this kind was also at the centre of an ambassadors' conference which – jointly with the federal minister for trade and industry, Otto Mitterer – I called in Vienna for 7 and 8 November 1968, and which was attended by the heads of the Austrian missions accredited to the EEC member states as well as the head of the Austrian mission to the European communities. The outcome of the negotiations was that these trade arrangements, if realized, would mean a certain degree of relief for Austria's exports to the Common Market and would also mean that such arrangements contained no political implications that were incompatible with Austria's international position. The ambassadors were therefore instructed to emphasize once again to their host governments

Austria's interest in participating in trade arrangements – as a provisional settlement pending the greater solution that Austria still hoped for.

However, these plans did not meet with the reception expected by Austria within the EEC. Although at the meeting of the EEC Council of Ministers on 4 and 5 November 1968 Debré once more supported the Franco-German proposals, differences of opinion between the member states concerning their compatibility with Gatt, the ultimate aims of the agreements and the identity of the participating countries could not be surmounted. A particularly critical attitude was adopted by the Netherlands, who gave priority to Britain's admission to the European communities and doubted whether the trade arrangements were compatible with Gatt. Italy, for her part, clung to the doctrine of association she had evolved in 1964 and wanted to conclude trade agreements only with candidates for membership. Agreement was reached solely on the point that the trade arrangements should not be a substitute for accession. No decision was taken by the EEC; still less was an offer made to the Efta states. From April 1969 onwards the arrangements for trade policy faded into the background, though without having been officially abandoned.

In the meantime France's attitude to the widening of the EEC by the admission of new members had become more flexible. The impression was gaining ground that French diplomacy, until recently reserved on the issue of the extension of the EEC, had started moving again and was genuinely trying to reactivate the discussion in order to find a way out of the *impasse* in which the Community had been since the second French veto of Britain's admission in December 1967.

These tendencies, which were at first only suspected, emerged clearly after the change in the French presidency and in the composition of the French government in July 1969. The decisive turning-point came at the meeting of the EEC Council of Ministers on 22 and 23 July, at which the French government spontaneously placed new emphasis on the integration and extension debate and at which it was decided, at France's suggestion, that a summit conference of the heads of state and heads of government of the Six should be held before the end of 1969. The Commission and the committee of permanent representatives were simultaneously instructed to re-examine their data on the enlargement of the Community and bring them up to date.

This meant that the policy of European integration was entering into a new phase, though for the time being no conclusions could be drawn as to its likely development over the next few months. Observers tended to show caution and restraint in their assessment of the prospects. In view of this uncertain development the Austrian government found themselves faced with the necessity of re-examining Austria's position on European integration and defining their line of advance for the future shaping of her relationship with the European communities.

The inevitable starting-point was Austria's unaltered wish to participate in a pan-European customs-free zone, because this was the only course that would meet the requirements of a modern economic and foreign trade policy. Such participation in economic co-operation in Europe was limited by the obligations arising from the state treaty and from considerations relating to the law of neutrality and a policy of neutrality.

FIRST SUCCESSES

In order to clarify matters and to make sure that Austria could seize any opportunities that offered themselves, I conducted a number of talks with the foreign ministers of the EEC states – for instance with Debré during my official visit to Paris on 20 and 21 February 1969, and with the Belgian foreign minister, Pierre Harmel, in Vienna on 26 July 1969. These conversations, which I continued with all the EEC foreign ministers – on the French side the post was now held by Maurice Schumann – when I attended the United Nations General Assembly in New York in late September and early October, indicated that a number of EEC members did not regard a resumption of the Austrian application to the Community as impossible, in view of the re-emergence of the enlargement issue, provided that the new circumstances were taken into account.

The same purpose was served – in addition to diplomatic soundings in the capitals of the Six – by my official visit to London on 26 and 27 July 1969; here I found, both on the part of the prime minister, Harold Wilson, and the foreign secretary, Michael Stewart, real understanding for Austria's desire to be

E

considered during the impending developments without any discrimination in time. I invariably stressed this problem of simultaneity in the handling of applications for admission and Austria's request in my conversations with the EEC foreign ministers. In particular Debré, and later Schumann, showed the greatest understanding for Austria's request to the extent that during the subsequent enlargement debates within the Community France became a genuine champion of Austria and of the European neutrals generally.

At an ambassadors' conference that I called jointly with my ministerial colleague Otto Mitterer for the end of October 1969 in Vienna, the Austrian heads of missions to the EEC countries were instructed to point out to their host governments, even before the EEC summit conference, which had meanwhile been called for 1 and 2 December in The Hague, that Austria was hoping to be duly considered. Because of her international status, Austria, like other states, had not applied for admission to the Community but, in view of her traditional trade, she was anxious to reach a satisfactory settlement of her economic relations with the European communities.

In point of fact, the heads of state and the heads of government of the Six in The Hague not only approved of the opening of negotiations with the candidates for admission – Britain, Norway, Denmark and Ireland – but also foreshadowed the opening of talks with the other Efta states concerning their relations with the European communities as soon as negotiations with the candidates for admission had begun.[11] This decision was welcomed by the Austrian government,[12] even though a realistic assessment of future developments made it clear that even in the event of a positive outcome of the summit meeting of the Six, a great deal of time would elapse before the negotiations with the candidates for membership could begin, and even more with the candidates for non-membership.

For that reason the federal government conveyed to the EEC members at the beginning of November 1969 its request that, regardless of any decisions to be taken by the EEC summit conference on a global agreement, Austria was interested in an interim solution.

This time the EEC Council of Ministers reacted swiftly. In its meeting of 8 – 9 December 1969 – when Italy in view of the settlement of the South Tyrol issue, formally withdrew her 1967 veto against the further discussion of the Austrian application – it invited the Commission to submit to it forthwith a complete report on the state of relations between Austria and the Community. In order to prepare this report, the Commission had tentative talks in Brussels on 17 and 18 December 1969, with an Austrian delegation of officials who explained in great detail Austrian views on the possibilities of an economic interim solution. These views were directed towards a preferential customs and trade agreement that would be in conformity with the stipulations of Article XXIV of Gatt and would remain in force until a comprehensive general settlement had been achieved between the EEC and all neutral states.

As the first stage of this preferential interim agreement the Austrian side proposed a bilateral reduction of customs by 40, or at any rate by 30, per cent in the industrial sector, while on the agricultural sector a wish was expressed for pinpointed trade relief – especially in the livestock and dairy sector. At the same time it was emphasized that such an interim agreement must on no account impair Austria's economic relations with the remaining Efta countries.

On the basis of these contacts and of the Austrian clarification, the Commission submitted to the Council on 24 February 1970 the report it had asked for on the possibilities for an interim solution. It reached the conclusion that the Community could not escape negotiations with Austria but that it was inappropriate to reopen the former dossier, which raised a number of fundamental issues, when negotiations of greater scope would shortly be embarked upon; these might encounter the same problems in connection with other Efta member states which did not aspire to EEC membership either.

The Commission recommended that the Council of Ministers should work towards an interim settlement and examine its report without delay so that directives for negotiations might be worked out as soon as possible.

A few days before the submission of the Commission's report to the Council – to be precise, on 18 February 1970 – I had an extensive talk in Brussels with Pierre Harmel who promised his full support for the interim agreement requested by Austria. In a subsequent conversation with Jean Rey, the president of the

Commission of the European communities, and with Eduardo Martino, the Commission member responsible for external relations, both of whom had just returned from the Commission's meeting approving the report on an interim agreement with Austria, they both assured me of their support for speedy handling of the Commission's report by the EEC foreign ministers. This took place on 20 and 21 March 1970 when the Council of Ministers took note of the Commission's report and instructed the permanent representatives to examine it in detail.

When the Kreisky government came into office on 21 April Austria's efforts at integration were once more under way. At least the deadlock had been broken. Two doors were in fact opening for the aspirations of Austria's economy to participate in a large European market. One of them led to an interim agreement which was to achieve at least a partial removal of trade obstacles without prejudicing the second alternative, i.e. the total abolition of customs tariffs within the framework of a global solution between a future enlarged European Economic Community and the Efta states that did not wish to become a member of it.

From then onwards the Council dealt with the Austrian interim agreement at each of their sessions. On 21 July they invited the Commission to submit to them as soon as possible the draft of a negotiating brief for a partial interim agreement. They themselves undertook to examine the draft brief at their first autumn session and, if possible, to authorize the Commission to start negotiations. The outcome of these negotiations, the foreign ministers decided, would have to be supplemented in relation to the objective and the timetable of further tariff reductions as soon as the talks and negotiations with the remaining Efta countries, especially the neutrals, had revealed a sufficiently clear-cut trend – concerning their orientation towards a free-trade zone and customs union – to enable the agreement with Austria to be made and put into effect on the basis of Article XXIV, paragraphs 5–9, of Gatt.

This decision of the Council, which was of great importance to Austria, represented a compromise, proposed by the Dutch foreign minister, Joseph Luns, between the French and Dutch views on whether an interim agreement was compatible with Gatt.

But it was chiefly the Italian foreign minister, Aldo Moro, who championed Austria's case at this session.

With this decision all six EEC members vouched for a degree of priority for Austria. Even though the interim agreement – if the idea outlined by the Council on 21 July was realized – would not come into force until the EEC's negotiations with the neutral Efta states had begun to reveal the structure of the global agreement that was aimed at, this still meant that the interim agreement with Austria would come into force at a time when negotiations with these states were still in progress or when the global agreements were at the stage of ratification. It is obvious that Austria's exports had been granted a considerable advantage.

The draft brief ordered by the Council was approved by the Commission on 9 September and submitted to the Council two days later. The Council issued the appropriate negotiating brief at their meeting on 26 October.

Running parallel with this development – negotiations on the admission of Britain, Ireland, Norway and Denmark had meanwhile been opened – the EEC Council of Ministers now turned to the future comprehensive settlement of relations between the Community and the states which did not wish to become members of it. On the basis of Point 14 of the communiqué of the summit conference in The Hague on 21 July the EEC Council of Ministers invited the three neutral Efta states, as well as Portugal, Finland and Iceland, to talks in the autumn on the subject of their future relations with the Community. These talks were opened with the first three countries on 10 November of that year and with the others on 24 November. A new, decisive phase was beginning for these countries in their efforts to regulate their relations with the European Common Market in a satisfactory manner.

Following these talks the Council of Ministers authorized the Commission to start negotiations with the Efta countries who did not want to join the EEC, with a view to regulating their relations with the community on the basis of a free-trade zone. Negotiations with Austria were continued on the basis of this brief and eventually concluded by the signing of a free-trade agreement between the European Community and Austria in July 1972. Thus the objective of these talks, the establishment of a free-trade zone for industrial manufacture between Austria and the EEC, was successfully reached after many years of painstaking effort. Within the framework of this zone there is to be a progressive abolition of customs. Such a regulation was in line with Austria's economic interest to come to an agreement with the EEC, the more so as it not only represents Austria's principal trade partner but will also include important former Efta partners such as Britain. Moreover the formula of a free-trade zone befits Austria's international status in that it acknowledges her economic sovereignty without running counter either to the 1955 treaty or to her status as a permanently neutral state. In addition, Austria will participate in a residual Efta. A settlement of relations between the EEC and the Efta countries who did not wish to join it became particularly urgent in January 1972 when Britain, Ireland, Denmark and Norway signed agreements on their entry into the EEC. Under these agreements Britain, Ireland and Denmark become full members of the Community on 1 January 1973. In the case of Norway a plebiscite held in the autumn of 1972 did not ratify the agreement on the entry of Norway into the EEC.

There can be no doubt that Austria's international status imposes on her the obligation of proceeding on the issue of European economic integration in such a manner that a future settlement will be in accordance with the obligations arising from neutrality and from the state treaty. It is just these considerations that have guided all federal governments since Austria's earliest efforts to come to an agreement with the EEC. Austria was in the dilemma here that she regarded a closer association with the Common Market as desirable for economic reasons, since it is after all her traditional trade partner, while on the other hand the considerations already noted impose certain limitations on such an association.

The crucial question for a neutral state therefore lies in an assessment of how closely it may approach the EEC without in so doing jeopardizing the degree of sovereignty that is indispensable for the maintenance of its neutrality. It has to move between two extremes – a settlement that conforms to the norms of the community of states but not to its own neutrality; and a solution that conforms to neutrality but fails to take its economic requirements into account. The answer must lie somewhere between the two.

It is certainly not Austria's fault if her efforts to come to a special agreement have dragged on for so long. The delay was due quite simply to the European constellation, which only in 1972 allowed for such an enlargement of the Community. It is clear, moreover, that economic integration should not be confined to one part of Europe but should ultimately embrace all European countries. Pan-European economic co-operation must therefore continue to be the aim of all efforts along these lines, for the future of our continent will undoubtedly depend on a satisfactory solution of this problem. I have referred to the close connection between economics and politics. This is particularly true of Europe. If we succeed in solving the economic problems then we will have created the prerequisites for the healthy political development of our continent. And this – and this alone – is what the interests of the nations of Europe demand.

9

THE SOUTH TYROL

The problem of the South Tyrol dates from the end of the First World War, when the peace treaty of Saint-Germain-en-Laye assigned the region to Italy as far as the Brenner frontier.[1] Basically this act was merely a formal confirmation of the assurance given to Italy by Britain, France and Russia in the secret London Treaty of 26 April 1915, when Italy joined the war on the side of the Allies. Ever since 1919 Austria had opposed the separation of the South Tyrol with every means at her disposal. But she had limited her demands to the northern part of the region, between the Salurner Klause and the Brenner – in other words, to the German-speaking South Tyrol, the modern province of Bolzano. The southern sector from Laka Garda to Salurn, the modern province of Trento, which is almost entirely Italian-speaking, was not claimed by Austria in view of her support of the principle of self-determination for all nations. Italy justified its claim to the South Tyrol by pointing out that the Brenner was a natural frontier. Added to this were strategic considerations. From the ethnic point of view the claim was not tenable, since the region between Brenner and Salurn is inhabited almost exclusively by a German-speaking population. In 1910, when the last Austrian census before the separation of the South Tyrol was held, the region was inhabited by 235,000 German and Ladin speakers and only 7,000 Italians. The Ladin speakers represented a relatively small Rhaeto-Romance ethnic group living in a few valleys in the South Tyrol, about 13,000 of them in the Province of Bolzano and about 9,000 in the provinces of Trento and Belluno.

THE GRUBER – DE GASPERI AGREEMENT

It has been pointed out repeatedly that the cession of the German-speaking South Tyrol, which for centuries had belonged to Austria, was totally at variance with Woodrow Wilson's 'fourteen points', proclaimed at the beginning of 1918 as the basis for the future peace negotiations. The ruling of the Treaty of Saint-Germain caused regret not only in Austria but also in the West, as revealed in statements by Lloyd George after the First World War and by Sir Winston Churchill after the Second World War.

Contrary to the assurances given to the South Tyrolese by the Italian democratic government after the annexation of their country, the seizure of power by the Fascists marked the realization of Tolomei's notorious programme of Italianization. Notices in German were banned, schoolchildren were no longer allowed to be taught their German mother-tongue, whole municipalities were subordinated to state municipal secretaries, their autonomy was abolished and the entire administration was totally centralized.

In the course of the *rapprochement* between Hitler and Mussolini an agreement was reached in 1939 between Rome and Berlin, following Italy's urgent request, that provided for the expatriation of the German-speaking population of the South Tyrol into the German Reich. It is said that Mussolini demanded Hitler's approval of this population transfer as repayment for the debt he owed him for Italy's benevolent attitude at the time of Austria's occupation by Germany in March 1938. After the fall of the Fascist regime in Italy in 1943 the expatriation was suspended; by that time about 70,000 South Tyrolese had left the country.

After the end of the Second World War Austria again tried to achieve self-determination for the South Tyrol. In September 1945 the provisional state government addressed an appeal to the foreign ministers' conference in London, demanding a plebiscite in the German-speaking South Tyrol. It was pointed out in the appeal that the ceding of the area in 1919 had been justified exclusively on strategic grounds, in other words on grounds that no longer existed after the Second World War.

Any threat to Italy from the north had become illusory with the disappearance of German military potential. This appeal did not create much of a stir. Indeed the great powers took the view that no major alterations to frontiers corrections should be carried out at Italy's expense and also stated that the decision not to touch Italian territory had first been taken at the Moscow conference of foreign Ministers in 1943. On 30 April 1946 the Paris conference of foreign ministers eventually decided not to carry out any major changes to the frontier between Austria and Italy; the foreign ministers' deputies were instructed to listen to Austria's representatives only in relation to minor frontier rectifications. The Paris conference of foreign ministers thus confirmed the decision taken by the London conference in October 1945 not to make any frontier changes and to reject the Austrian demand for self-determination for South Tyrol. Numerous negotiations took place subsequently between the foreign ministers' deputies and representatives of Austria and Italy. Austria's foreign minister, Dr Karl Gruber, who as the leader of the Austrian delegation had done his best in tough negotiations to redress the wrong committed at Saint-Germain by negotiating the return of South Tyrol to Austria, was compelled to acknowledge that the great powers were not prepared to accept Austria's arguments. In May 1946, under the heading of 'frontier rectifications', he therefore demanded the surrender to Austria of a border region of 1,236 square miles with a population of about 70,000. This concerned the Pustertal (Val Pusteria) with the town of Bruneck (Brunico) and the Brixen (Bressanone) plain. Italy rejected this demand.

The Paris conference of foreign ministers in June 1946 again rejected the frontier changes proposed by Austria, on the grounds that they were not 'minor'. An important proposal was made by Britain – to attach to the peace treaty with Italy a clause to the effect that Italy should conduct negotiations with Austria for a satisfactory settlement of the problem of traffic communication in the border territory. This clause offered a chance of again raising the problem of the South Tyrol during the peace treaty conference with Italy. In these negotiations Austria again made desperate efforts to effect the application of the right of self-determination to South Tyrol. These efforts also failed. The Austrian delegation therefore had to decide whether to lodge a formal objection to the decision of the Paris conference or to try to achieve the greatest possible measure of autonomy for the province of Bolzano by way of direct negotiations with Italy. The latter course was chosen, in agreement with the representatives of the South Tyrol on the Austrian delegation. Following difficult negotiations an Austro-Italian agreement concerning the autonomy to be granted by Italy to the South Tyrol was reached in Paris on 5 September 1946. This document, signed by the two foreign ministers, Dr Karl Gruber and Alcide de Gasperi, came to be known as the Gruber–de Gasperi agreement. The autonomy envisaged in it comprised the German-speaking province of Bolzano, including the areas of the lower Bolzano region that had been incorporated into the province of Trento during the Fascist era. The region was given the official name of Alto Adige. The Austro-Italian agreement on the South Tyrol was incorporated into the Italian peace treaty as Annex IV. Article 85 of the treaty stipulates that the Annexes rank as integral parts of the peace treaty and have the same significance as the treaty itself. On 27 June 1947 the Italian parliament decided to set up a region called Trentino-Alto Adige. The South Tyrolese had not been consulted. This led to a series of sharp protests from the South Tyrolese against the amalgamation of the German-speaking province of Bolzano with the Italian province of Trentino to form a single region, but these protests had no effect.

In November 1947 an agreement was reached between Austria and Italy concerning a revision of the 'citizenship options' that had arisen on the basis of the Hitler–Mussolini agreement of 1939. The 'option decree' issued by Italy on the basis of this agreement enabled the South Tyrolese who had opted for Germany at the time to be repatriated into Italy, in other words to return to South Tyrol.

THE STATUTE OF AUTONOMY

The statute of autonomy for the Trentino-Alto Adige region came into force in March 1948. The creation of this statute triggered off decades of disputes between Austria and Italy and these seriously upset the otherwise fruitful relations between the two countries. Austria failed to understand why Italy should choose to interpret the Paris agreement in a way that made the

South Tyrol not a region on its own but part of a predominantly Italian-speaking region. True, the statute of autonomy did grant the South Tyrol autonomy – but this was autonomy at the provincial level, not 'regional autonomy'. In all regional matters South Tyrol had to work together with Trento, with the result that on the more important questions the South Tyrolese deputies did not have a parliamentary majority. This legislative arrangement was endorsed in the most literal sense by the centralized judiciary of the Italian constitutional court. In the Austrian view, on the other hand, the purpose of the Paris agreement had been to ensure autonomy for the South Tyrol alone and not for a region with a predominantly Italian-speaking population. In numerous interventions Austria therefore pointed out the absurdity of this arrangement to the Italian government, though her entirely logical arguments failed to make any impression.

A great deal of friction between Austria and Italy and a great deal of terrorism and unhappiness in the South Tyrol could have been avoided if the Italian government had decided to apply more promptly a generous or at least a logical interpretation to the Paris agreement. Such concessions as were eventually made by the Italian side after laborious negotiations might well, if they had been made sooner, have had a far more favourable effect on relations between the two countries and also on relations between the South Tyrolese minority and the Italian authorities. In fact it took years of stubborn negotiations between the two governments, an approach to the United Nations, the efforts of the Council of Europe and finally renewed direct negotiations to achieve a compromise solution which would ensure that the South Tyrolese could preserve their ethnic character and their cultural and economic development.

Whereas from 1946 to 1949 Austria's South Tyrol policy was concerned predominantly with a solution of the option issue, the next task was to ensure that the autonomous rights envisaged in the Gruber–de Gasperi agreement were in fact granted to the South Tyrolese. This required the regulations giving effect to the statute of autonomy. The draft of these, however, was very soon withdrawn from the competence of the parity commission, on which the South Tyrolese were also represented, and transferred to a new commission under the chairmanship of state council-lor Innocenti. The enactment of these regulations was constantly being delayed, so the Austrian government was eventually com-pelled to initiate various steps and interventions in Rome to ensure the observation of the Paris agreement, especially in relation to the new restrictive regulations. At the same time the federal government proposed the setting up of a mixed Austro-Italian commission to work for a solution of the outstanding questions. When these efforts misfired, Gruber demanded in a note to the three western powers on 18 October 1953 that a plebiscite should be held in South Tyrol. In the following year the South Tyrolese deputies, greatly concerned about the imple-mentation of the Paris agreement, submitted to the Italian government a memorandum in which the South Tyrolese re-quests and complaints were set out in detail. This step again produced no results – any more than did the Austrian govern-ment's repeated inquiries about the state of negotiations between Rome and the South Tyrolese. On 8 October 1956 the Austrian federal government eventually handed the Italian government a memorandum in which the Austrian complaints about the non-observance of the Paris agreement by Italy were set out in detail. Simultaneously, Austria once more proposed the setting up of a mixed commission of experts to examine all controversial ques-tions arising from the Paris agreement and to submit proposals to the two governments within a definite period of time. The Italian memorandum sent in reply to this rejected the proposals for a mixed commission of experts and instead suggested that the differences should be cleared up through the normal diplomatic channels.

When further Austrian efforts proved equally unsuccessful, the South Tyrolese People's Party moved a proposal in the Italian chamber of deputies in February 1958 for a statute of autonomy to be granted specifically for the region of South Tyrol, whereby the province of Bolzano was to receive full auton-omy independently of the province of Trento. On 26 September 1958 the Tyrol Diet (in Austria) passed a resolution supporting the separate regional autonomy demanded by the South Tyrolese for the province of Bolzano. This resolution by the Tyrol Diet underlined the close collaboration between the Austrian federal government and the provincial government of the Tyrol, which has been particularly characteristic of Austria's South Tyrol policy ever since.

INTERVENTION BY THE UNITED NATIONS

On 4 March 1959 Leopold Figl reported to the Austrian National Assembly on developments concerning the South Tyrol question. The National Assembly invited the federal government by a unanimous resolution to take all possible measures to ensure the full implementation of the Paris agreement. On 21 September, following a government reshuffle, the new Austrian foreign minister, Dr Bruno Kreisky, raised the South Tyrol issue in the UN General Assembly. He referred to the differences of opinion that had arisen over the interpretation of the Paris agreement and to the many years of fruitless negotiations. Only the establishment of an autonomous South Tyrol, he stated, could bring about a genuine implementation of the Paris agreement. If bilateral negotiations continued to prove fruitless the federal government would have to apply to the United Nations. The Italian foreign minister, Giuseppe Pella, retorted that the issue was an internal Italian matter over which the UN had no jurisdiction.

Since it proved impossible to settle the question by negotiation, the Austrian government decided to raise it at the United Nations General Assembly in 1960. Following very fierce argument from both sides in the special political committee of the General Assembly a resolution was eventually unanimously adopted in which both contesting parties were instructed to resume negotiations with the aim of finding a solution of all differences relating to the implementation of the Paris agreement. If these negotiations did not produce a satisfactory result within a reasonable period of time, the two parties would have to seek a solution of their differences by one of the peaceful means envisaged in the UN charter – either in the international court or by some other means chosen by themselves. The resolution finally recommended that the contesting parties should abstain from any action that might impair their friendly relations.

This resolution, as Kreisky pointed out, was valuable to Austria chiefly because it recognized her right to discuss the South Tyrol issue with Italy. Until then Italy had disputed that right, regarding the question as an Italian domestic problem. This line of argument was no longer possible. A further advantage of the resolution was that it authorized the contestants to choose the peaceful means envisaged in the charter in the event of bilateral negotiations failing to produce positive results. In the past Italy had insisted that in the event of a dispute the international court alone would be competent to make a ruling. The preamble to the resolution was also particularly valuable. It included the paragraphs that reflected most clearly the spirit of the Paris agreement – the point that the German-speaking population should be guaranteed complete equality with the Italian population within the framework of special regulations designed to protect the ethnic character and the cultural and economic advancement of the German-speaking element.

In line with this resolution of the UN General Assembly a number of negotiations were conducted in 1961 and 1962 at foreign minister and expert level in Milan, Klagenfurt and Zurich. The Austrian delegation was headed by Dr Kreisky and his state secretary, Professor Franz Gschnitzer, while Italy's case was argued by her foreign minister, Antonio Segni. Yet in spite of the most intensive efforts it proved impossible to achieve any concrete results in these negotiations or to ensure regional autonomy for the province of Bolzano.

Thus on 5 July 1961 Dr Kreisky stated in the National Assembly that he considered that the bilateral negotiation brief of the United Nations had been exhausted in view of the Italian government's refusal to discuss the implementation of regional autonomy for Bolzano in the spirit of the Paris agreement. It was therefore necessary, in line with the UN resolution, to seek a solution of the problem by other peaceful means. The Austrian government had accordingly proposed to Rome either the setting up of an international commission of inquiry to examine conditions on the spot or, as an alternative, mediation by the UN secretary general in the choice of the peaceful procedure to be adopted. On 7 July the Italian government rejected this proposal and proposed instead that the question should be submitted to the international court. Austria therefore once more asked for it to be placed on the agenda of the UN General Assembly.

TERRORISM AND NEW NEGOTIATIONS

Meanwhile the situation had become exacerbated by a series of bombing attacks in South Tyrol. Austria dissociated herself unequivocally from these outrages and invariably condemned the pursuit of political aims by violent means, but in July 1961 the Italian government imposed passport and visa restrictions on Austrians travelling to Italy. This step was justified by the argument that the Austrian government had failed to take the necessary measures to prevent the smuggling of explosives into Italy or the planning of such attacks from Austrian territory. The federal government protested against these unfounded accusations, but the Italian government still accused Austria of complicity in the bombing outrages. In a note of 1 August 1961 Vienna repudiated these accusations in the strongest terms and proposed that an international commission of inquiry should be set up or that the incidents should be investigated by the UN secretary general.

The Italian government now took a step that was to prove to be the decisive turning-point in the negotiations over the South Tyrol. On 13 September 1961 Rome appointed a mixed commission to deal with the South Tyrol issue. The commission consisted of nineteen members and was made up of parliamentary deputies and political experts, including seven members of the South Tyrolese People's Party. It was headed by the vice-president of the Italian Chamber, the Social Democrat deputy Paolo Rossi. Over many years of joint efforts by Italian and South Tyrolese experts this 'commission of nineteen' laid the foundation for the rights subsequently granted to the province of Bolzano in what became known as the 'package'.

In the autumn of 1961, however, before the commission began its work, the UN General Assembly again dealt with the question, at Austria's request. The federal government pointed out in a memorandum that the Austro-Italian negotiations envisaged in the General Assembly's resolution of 31 October 1960 had not produced any results. The General Assembly was therefore requested, in line with the second section of its resolution of 31 October 1960, to assist the contesting parties in choosing another peaceful method of solving the problem. The Italian government thereupon notified the General Assembly in a white paper of the terrorist attacks in the South Tyrol and attributed a share in the responsibility for them to Austria. During the discussion of the issue in the special political committee of the General Assembly Kreisky proposed the setting up of an international commission for the problem in line with the European convention on the peaceful settlement of disputes. He rejected in the strongest terms the Italian accusations of Austrian complicity in the bombing outrages.

The tactics of the Italian delegation, under the leadership of their foreign minister, Antonio Segni, involved describing the bilateral negotiations between Austria and Italy as not yet concluded. An international commission, as proposed by Austria, could not therefore be considered, but the Rome government was prepared to bring about a satisfactory solution to the problem by way of the commission of nineteen that had already been appointed. In this way Italy attempted to support her standpoint that the problem was an Italian internal matter, a point of view that was by no means shared by Austria. On 28 October 1961 the sixteenth General Assembly, after a lengthy debate, eventually adopted a resolution which once more called upon the contesting parties to direct their efforts towards solving the problem in the spirit of their earlier resolution.

Thus the General Assembly's second resolution merely represented a confirmation of their first resolution of 1960. Yet it was important to Austria to have her international negotiating brief confirmed, in view of the fact that Italy – as already mentioned – continued to represent the South Tyrol problem as a purely internal matter in which Austria had no right whatever to intervene. Vienna's objections that Austria's protective role *vis-à-vis* the South Tyrolese stemmed from an international treaty, i.e. the Gruber–de Gasperi agreement of 1946, were countered with the argument that Italy's obligations arising from that agreement had already been discharged and that Austria's claim to intervention on the strength of the Paris agreement had therefore expired. Austria was unable to accept this point of view and instead the Vienna government emphatically pointed out that the

Paris agreement had not been implemented because Italy had interpreted it in a totally one-sided manner. They added that Austria, as a partner in the Paris agreement, had not only the right but indeed the duty to look after the interests of the South Tyrolese.

THE SOUTH TYROL ISSUE BEFORE THE COUNCIL OF EUROPE

In view of the as yet unclarified situation and the increasing exacerbation of relations between Austria and Italy the Council of Europe in Strasbourg, of which both contesting parties were members, began to concern itself with the South Tyrol problem. In his capacity as chairman of the political commission of the consultative assembly of the Council of Europe, Paul Struye, president of the Belgian Senate, held intermediary talks in Vienna and Rome on the instructions of a newly created sub-committee for the South Tyrol. In a report to the sub-committee Struye stated that in his view the work of the Italian commission on the South Tyrol (the 'commission of nineteen') was making satisfactory progress and that he therefore proposed that discussion of the problem should be suspended until the Italian commission had completed its work. Meanwhile fresh fuel was being added to the flames by reports of South Tyrolese detainees being tortured in Italian prisons. Italy promised a judicial inquiry into these incidents. Austria pointed out that evidence was available that gravely incriminated Italian law-enforcement agencies.

A further meeting between the Austrian and Italian foreign ministers in Venice on 31 July 1962 resulted in a certain easing of tension in their relations. Austria acknowledged the fundamental importance of the commission of nineteen in view of the fact that those directly affected, i.e. the South Tyrolese, were taking part in its work. In the light of these developments Austria agreed not to put the problem on the agenda of the impending UN General Assembly. In September 1962 the Italian government thereupon rescinded the compulsory visa for Austrians. During the period that followed the Austrian government – irrespective of the work of the commission of nineteen – endeavoured to achieve some progress on the matter of regional autonomy for the province of Bolzano by means of negotiations with Italy. The United Nations General Assemblies during that period heard reports from both delegations on the state of the negotiations, Austria noting with regret that they were dragging on and that Italy was avoiding another meeting of foreign ministers. The Italian foreign minister, Attilio Piccioni, justified the delay in the negotiations on technical grounds, chiefly the elections being held in Austria and Italy. In October 1963 another meeting between Kreisky and Piccioni was finally held in Geneva and it was decided that the negotiations should be continued through diplomatic channels. Meanwhile the commission of nineteen had essentially completed its report, which was to serve as the basis for future Austro-Italian contacts. An important agreement was reached to the effect that the divergent views of the South Tyrolese, i.e. the minority views, should be included in the commission's report.

The commission completed its report in the spring of the following year and handed it to the Italian premier, Aldo Moro. It proposed a series of measures designed to grant the South Tyrolese additional legislative and executive rights. Legislative rights for the province of Bolzano were recommended to be chiefly in the field of agriculture and forestry, tourism, education, trade and public health, hospital administration, etc. The report also envisaged equal status for the German and Italian languages as well as an ethnic ratio in the filling of public offices. Without any doubt the report represented a step forward in the efforts to work out a peaceful settlement of the problem. Regrettably, however, the Italian and South Tyrolese members of the commission had failed to agree on proposals covering a great number of points and this gave rise to many years of arguments.

Silvius Magnago, the provincial governor of the South Tyrol and chairman of the South Tyrolese People's Party, made it clear when signing the report that the recommendations that had been made without the agreement of the South Tyrolese could not be binding upon them. In a resolution of 21 May 1964 the People's Party pointed out that the wish of the South Tyrolese to see the creation of an autonomous region of the South Tyrol was based on the letter and spirit of the Paris agreement. Even though the recommendations of the commission had failed to fulfil this hope, the South Tyrolese members were prepared, in order to reach agreement at long last, to accept the regional framework of autonomy as existing at present, on condition that the province of Bolzano was furnished with the legislative and executive rights that related to the ethnic, cultural and economic life of the South Tyrolese. At the same time they expressed regret that the commission had failed to take a number of well-founded South Tyrolese demands into account.[2]

At a meeting in Geneva between the two foreign ministers, Kreisky and Saragat, on 25 May 1964 it was agreed to set up a mixed commission of experts from both countries. Its task was to be the clarification of those aspects of the South Tyrolese problem that were as yet unsolved. The committee held a number of meetings lasting until October 1964. In between – on 7 and 8 September – came a further meeting in Geneva between Kreisky and Saragat, who were able to establish, thanks to the progress made in the negotiations among the experts, that there had been a marked *rapprochement* in the two sides' points of view.

The favourable climate of the negotiations in Geneva encouraged the hope that after all these years a more or less satisfactory settlement of the problem might yet be achieved. But a new wave of terrorism in South Tyrol seriously disrupted the talks. There was vehement comment in the mass media on both sides, with the Austrian press observing that extremist elements were clearly trying to prevent the South Tyrol problem being settled whenever a *rapprochement* was in sight. The federal chancellor, Josef Klaus, addressed an appeal to the people who were allowing themselves to be swept into terrorist activities from a mistaken sense of patriotism; they must realize the gravity of the situation and refrain from any kind of violence. Bruno Kreisky observed that the actions of the terrorists ran counter to the true interests of the South Tyrolese population, since they were designed to sabotage a peaceful solution. The Austrian government categorically condemned acts of violence and unreservedly supported the 1960 resolution of the UN General Assembly.

A further exchange of views between Kreisky and Saragat took place in Paris on 16 December 1964. Both of them pointed to the far-reaching *rapprochement* that had been achieved in negotiations among the experts. Whereas agreement was reached in substance on the issue of the international 'anchoring' of the 'package' of measures being offered by Italy to the South Tyrol, a number of unfulfilled Austrian requirements concerning the nature of these measures failed to meet with Italy's approval.

The anchoring formula envisaged in December 1964 foresaw the establishment of an arbitration body consisting of two adjudicators each appointed by Italy and Austria, plus one neutral; this body was to have jurisdiction over disputes concerning the interpretation of bilateral agreements. The arbitration body was also to be authorized to verify over a five-year period whether the measures envisaged in the 'package' had been put into effect by Italy. Thus as far as the 'package' itself was concerned, the arbitration commission would merely judge facts and not issue instructions. In other words it would merely establish if necessary Italy's failure to fulfil certain promises, without being able to order her to implement such measures. The term of office of this arbitration commission on the 'package' was limited to five years.

Although a great many points had been cleared up in the experts' negotiations about the nature of the measures offered by Italy for the South Tyrol, a number of important Austrian requests had remained open. On most of these points the foreign ministers' meeting in Paris in December 1964 also failed to produce agreement.

There can be no doubt that the arrangement envisaged in December 1964 represented a definite step forward in the settlement of the South Tyrol problem and that it probably represented the maximum attainable at that point in time and in the particular circumstances.

The non-acceptance by Italy of a number of important demands was the reason why the Italian offer of December 1964 did not meet with the approval of the representatives of the South Tyrolese ethnic group at a discussion in Innsbruck on 8 January 1965. This meeting decided that the South Tyrolese People's Party should continue to try to obtain further substantial improvements by way of direct contacts with the Italian government. The first talks along these lines were held by the South Tyrolese and the Italian premier, Aldo Moro, in March 1965. They provided an opportunity for the South Tyrolese members of parliament to set before the Italian premier the questions that had remained open in the commission of nineteen and in bilateral Austro-Italian negotiations. They left him in no doubt that unless these questions were solved a final regulation of the problem could not be approved.

Austria's efforts were continuing at the same time on the bilateral plane. The two main issues, as they had been in the negotiations of experts in 1964, were the following:

1. the solution of those questions in the 'package' that had not been satisfactorily settled either by the commission of nineteen or in the bilateral talks between experts;

2. a formula for the implementation and international 'anchoring' of the Italian promises.

These were the two issues that prevented a solution of the problem over the next few years. Italy was not prepared to meet all the wishes of the South Tyrolese. True, they did make some partial concessions, but on a number of major points agreement still could not be reached. In this situation the Austrian federal government endeavoured to enrich the 'package' through the diplomatic channels and in bilateral negotiations and there were also direct contacts between the provincial governor of the South Tyrol and the Italian premier. These determined efforts by the Austrians and the South Tyrolese remained unsuccessful for a considerable time. Talks between the federal chancellor and the Italian foreign minister and acting president of the UN General Assembly, Amintore Fanfani, and with President Segni and Aldo Moro, the prime minister, during the Vatican Council's celebrations in Rome in December 1965 again failed to bring about any change of heart on the Italian side. It was realized that although the parties had come very close to a sensible settlement, there was a danger that it might yet be wrecked by the last of the unresolved questions.

THE 'PACKAGE' AND ITS TIMETABLE

Over the next few years efforts were therefore made in a number of confidential talks between experts to break out of the deadlocked negotiations. These negotiations, which mostly took place in London, were concerned with trying to improve the 'package' and with the question of an international 'anchoring', i.e. of insuring the 'package' against its possible non-implementation by Italy. Once a number of improvements concerning the contents of the package had been achieved in bilateral negotiations with

Italy, the provincial governor and chairman of the South Tyrolese People's Party, Silvius Magnago, succeeded in obtaining further Italian concessions in personal conversations with Signor Moro. On 23 March 1967 the executive of the People's Party decided to recommend to the party congress that the package should be accepted as soon as a formula had been found by Austria and Italy for an 'effective international anchoring' of the promises outlined in the package.

On the issue of anchoring, the non-acceptance of the global offer made by the Italian foreign minister, Giuseppe Saragat, in December 1964 had induced the Italian side to withdraw its agreement to the anchoring formula envisaged jointly by Kreisky and Saragat. Following the elections to the Austrian National Assembly in 1966 and the formation of a new federal government, Dr Kreisky's successor to the post of foreign minister, Dr Lujo Tončić-Sorinj, tried to get the negotiations going again. The main problem was how to find a way out of the dilemma of legal concepts on both sides. Whereas Italy continued to hold the view that the Italian concessions contained in the package were an internal matter with which Austria had no legal title to concern herself, the Austrian government declared that the package represented an act implementing the Paris agreement. Attempts by the foreign ministry in Vienna to solve the problem by actions establishing a *fait accompli* were unsuccessful. In fact the situation was becoming, if anything, even more complicated, since from now on the Italian government suspected that all the Austrian attempts to solve the question of guaranteeing or ensuring the package were really attempts to internationalize the South Tyrol problem.

This then was the situation when I took over the Austrian foreign ministry in 1968. My first aim was to reduce the existing feeling of suspicion and to convince Italy that the Austrian federal government was seriously interested in bringing the negotiations to an end. This was no easy task, since this distrust was deeply rooted on both sides. By dint of much laborious and detailed work I eventually managed to create the necessary conditions for a new round of negotiations. The starting-point was that each negotiating party would cling to its legal interpretation; the problem was to be clarified in a pragmatic manner. The result was the 'package and timetable'.

Here is a short outline of the course that these negotiations took; they did not lack a certain dramatic element and constantly seemed to be on the verge of breakdown. Whereas fundamental agreement did exist between Austria and Italy, on the basis of the positive resolution made by the executive of the South Tyrolese People's Party in March 1967, on the substance of the package, i.e. the Italian measures for the South Tyrol, the opposing points of view over the legal aspect of the measures in the package had proved irreconcilable in spite of years of effort. Yet the interests of the South Tyrolese ethnic group demanded that any possible opportunity of improving the autonomy of the South Tyrol should be seized, regardless of the legal title under which Italy was prepared to grant this new autonomy. Attempts were therefore made, leaving aside the controversial legal views, to work out a timetable that would lead to the implementation of the measures envisaged for the South Tyrol, to the ending of the dispute that was still pending with the United Nations, and finally to the emergence of an agreement that would settle any future disputes between the two states in international law. The basic concept underlying this timetable was the fact that due implementation of the package by Italy represented the condition for Austria's declaration that the dispute was at an end and for the coming into force of the 'international court agreement'.[3] An important point here was the clarification agreed in the bilateral negotiations that, following the withdrawal of the arbitration authority envisaged in the proposal of 1964, it was now up to Austria to judge whether the package had been properly implemented and thus when the dispute should be declared to be at an end and the international court agreement could come into force.

The question as to what stage of the implementation of the package would be appropriate for the Austrian declaration that the dispute was over was the subject of bilateral talks between experts. Whereas the Italians had originally wanted it to be agreed that this should take place as soon as the constitutional law changing the autonomy statute for the South Tyrol and the other laws had been adopted, Austria succeeded, during the experts talks, in gaining acceptance for her view that the dispute could not be declared over, nor could the international court agreement come into force until the regulations had been issued that would give effect to the constitutional law, along with certain administrative provisions and a decree concerning the transfer of offices and personnel from the Trentino-South Tyrol region to the province of Bolzano.

In arranging the sequence of the various points provided for in the timetable it was very important to achieve a balance in the steps to be taken by both sides. Austria and Italy agreed that each step to be taken by one partner must depend on the due implementation by the other partner of the preceding action. Mutual interest in the collateral expected from the other side thus became a kind of mainspring for the smooth running of the timetable, and had to be a substitute for the unattainable 'anchoring' of the package under international law.

The favourable progress of the Austro-Italian experts' negotiations during 1968 and 1969, which took place in an entirely correct atmosphere, was not invariably smooth or free from delays and reverses. Although the bilateral meetings of experts were interrupted during the first six months of 1968 by parliamentary elections and the formation of a new government in Italy, there were no fewer than five meetings of experts between July and December of the same year, most of them in Paris. As a preparation for these meetings many consultations were held with the provincial governors and other representatives of the (Austrian) North Tyrol and the South Tyrol, in which the line to be followed by the Austrian experts was laid down.

Towards the end of January 1969, just as the bilateral negotiations appeared to be approaching agreement following another round of experts' talks, an unexpected major delay occurred. This was connected with the contents of the package, a question that, it was thought, had been basically settled in 1967. A comparison of the package text prepared in March 1967 by the South Tyrolese People's Party, on the strength of direct contacts with the Italian government, and that of the Italian government revealed a large number of discrepancies. Although most of these were cleared up by renewed contacts between the South Tyrolese People's Party and the Italian government, a hard core of twelve unsolved points required several more months of intensive efforts on the political plane before the Italian government took a decision on the outstanding points of the package on 25 June 1969. The chances of reaching an agreement, though it was now clearly within reach, seemed to be snatched away again a few days later when a government crisis erupted in Italy following a split in the Socialist Party. Fortunately this pessimistic view proved to be unfounded, since the caretaker government announced that it was willing to continue the negotiations with Austria. Thus at the end of July 1969 the final meeting of experts took place in Paris and the remaining problems concerning the timetable – chiefly the question of when the international court agreement was to be signed – were settled in a way that was satisfactory to Austria.

The technical agreement reached by the experts and the handing over of the final package text to Magnago at the end of September 1969 meant that after many years of negotiations a proposal for solving the South Tyrol problem had been worked out that envisaged the implementation of a package in accordance with a bilateral timetable.

This package of measures for the South Tyrol listed a total of 137 points, which were to be implemented at different legislative levels. At the constitutional law level about three-quarters of the measures provided for amendments and supplements to the existing autonomy statute for Trentino-South Tyrol; according to these the majority of the rights formerly belonging to the region, as well as a number of rights formerly vested in the state, were transferred to the provinces of Bolzano and Trento. The most important of the new rights granted to the South Tyrol were in the economic sphere and in that of public order, but others concerned the cultural sector. Thus the province of Bolzano was given the right to legislate in the field of transport and communications, water supplies, tourism and the catering industry, agriculture and trade. The right to challenge state legislation on the grounds of infringement of the autonomy statute, was now granted to the provinces, whereas formerly it had been restricted to the region. The provincial governor was now entitled to take part in the meetings of the Italian Council of Ministers whenever questions concerning the South Tyrol were discussed. Participation in regional and provincial elections required four years' residence, two of them within the province. In the education sector the new autonomy statute provided for a director of education for the German-speaking schools, to be appointed by the provincial government and not subject to the Italian superintendent of schools. On the subject of language the package included the principle of equality for German and Italian, as well as the express possibility of a separate use of both languages. Public posts were to be filled – with certain exceptions – on a proportional basis between the ethnic groups, i.e. in accordance with the size of the separate language groups.

At the same time a number of important Austrian or South Tyrolese demands, especially in the field of public security, the right of domicile and employment, were not met, or only partially met in spite of years of efforts.

In addition to the reorganization of the autonomy statute at the constitutional level the package also contained a number of regulations that gave effect to the constitutional law, certain other laws (including the right of the province to prepare an economic development plan and the decentralization of municipal secretaries) and some administrative provisions.

The timetable contained a total of eighteen points. The most important covered the government declarations to be made to its parliament by each side and the resolutions to be adopted on them; the question of Austria's declaration of the termination of the dispute; the international court agreement, including the steps that were to precede its coming into force (initialling, signature and parliamentary approval); and notification of the United Nations. At the end of the timetable, as a token of a new era in Austro-Italian relations, provision is made for the possibility of a treaty on friendly co-operation being signed.

At first the Austro-Italian agreement on the regulation of the South Tyrol problem was a purely technical one. A great many political decisions were required before the settlement could be implemented. During the experts' negotiations Austria had always made it quite clear that the envisaged settlement would be acceptable to the Austrian government only if it was approved by the elected representatives of the South Tyrolese ethnic group. On 20 October 1969 the executive of the South Tyrolese People's Party recommended acceptance of the package and timetable by the party congress by forty-one votes to twenty-three, with two abstentions. After several weeks of campaigning in the various districts of the South Tyrol the congress was held in Merano on 22 November 1969, and after many hours of lively discussion it decided in favour of the proposed plan, with 52.9 per cent of the votes in favour, 44.5 per cent against and 2.6 per cent abstentions. The decision on the South Tyrol issue provided the basis for the necessary decisions to be made on the international plane for the implementation of the proposed plan. On 30 November a political agreement between Austria and Italy on the package and timetable was announced at a meeting of their foreign ministers in Copenhagen.

My meeting in Copenhagen with Signor Moro, the last of a series of meetings which involved his predecessors Giuseppe Medici and Pietro Nenni, gave me an opportunity to raise with my Italian colleague a number of further questions above and beyond the South Tyrol problem proper – chiefly the Austrian request for an amnesty for the South Tyrolese detainees. Signor Moro promised that these questions would be sympathetically examined. The Austro-Italian agreement in Copenhagen was the signal for the timetable to be put in motion and thus for the package to be implemented. The international court agreement (item 1 of the operations calendar) was initialled in Vienna on 2 December and was followed soon afterwards by the issuing of the administrative provisions listed in the timetable (item 2) and by a declaration by the Italian government to the Chamber and Senate, together with their resolution in favour of it (3 to 5 December).

On 15 December the federal chancellor, Dr Klaus, made the declaration on the South Tyrol to the Austrian National Assembly, as envisaged under item 4 of the timetable. After reviewing the way in which the problem had evolved and the decades of negotiations, he commented on the proposed settlement, declaring at the same time that during the period envisaged for the implementation of the package (a period of about four years) the Austrian government would not take the South Tyrol problem to any international body. On 16 December after a lively debate lasting several hours, during which I repeatedly had the opportunity to answer questions from members of the House, the National Assembly passed a resolution on the lines of the government declaration by eighty-three votes to seventy-nine.

The same day a decree by the Italian premier set up a preparatory committee (envisaged under item 5 of the timetable) of nine people (including two South Tyrolese), which was to assist the government in drafting the constitutional and other necessary laws. Within a few weeks the preparatory committee had worked out the draft of the constitutional law for the re-organization of the autonomy statute of the Trentino-South Tyrol region; it was presented to the Chamber of Deputies by the government on 19 January 1970, i.e. in advance of the deadline envisaged for it. In a resolution of 26 January the executive of the South Tyrolese People's Party expressed its approval of this draft constitutional law and voiced a hope that the Italian parliament would now pass the constitutional law and the other outstanding laws as a matter of urgency and in accordance with the package.

While we do not deny that the agreed settlement is not an ideal solution – we had searched in vain for such a solution for fifty years – I am convinced that it represents the best possible agreement in the circumstances. It seems to me that on the basis of this agreement measures should be enacted as a matter of urgency to enable the South Tyrolese to preserve their essential character; that, after all, is what we expect of this plan. There is not the slightest doubt that the severance of the South Tyrol from Austria after the end of the First World War amounted to a blatant violation of the right of nations to self-determination and was one of those historical mistakes from which the people of our continent have suffered so severely. The strategic considerations put forward by the Italian side at the time carry scarcely any weight in this nuclear age. It was therefore all the more discouraging to find the Allied powers clinging to this decision after the Second World War. Austria made desperate efforts to remedy this injustice and to negotiate a settlement for the South Tyrol in line with the principles of the United Nations charter and the right of nations to self-determination. This did not prove possible and it soon resulted in a serious worsening of relations between Italy and Austria. In the end we had to bow to a development the detrimental effects of which were only too predictable, though we had fought against them in vain. The settlement that was eventually reached represents a compromise; it was designed, by means of full autonomy for the province of Bolzano, to preserve the character of an ethnic group that had belonged to Austria for centuries; it was also intended to bring about peaceful coexistence between the South Tyrolese and the Italian majority.

On the South Tyrol issue, as on any other issue, it was ultimately necessary to think in terms of realistic politics and not to indulge in illusions that might have had disastrous consequences for the minority concerned.

Needless to say, this settlement does not mean that Austria's protective role has expired; after all, the Paris agreement is still in force. Austria will therefore continue to fulfil this role accordingly in the future. Should the agreement fail, Austria will still be able to use all the various political channels for raising the problem. All we can do is to express the earnest hope that the arrangement will be faithfully implemented on both sides and that it will prove possible to settle the South Tyrol problem in a European spirit, thereby providing the opportunity for peaceful and trusting coexistence for all sections of the population.

10

THE POLICY IN THE DANUBE REGION

Both Austria's past and her future, or in other words our destiny, are closely linked with the Danube region and are vitally affected by events in the neighbouring countries. This was as true for the Austro-Hungarian monarchy as it was for the first and second republics. Not only is Austria situated at the intersection of the Germanic, Slav and Latin worlds with their diverse ethnic, cultural and other features, but since the Second World War she has also been at the point where the two great ideological spheres of influence meet.

In spite of the considerable differences within the relatively narrow geographic concept of the 'Danube region', the countries in the region are closely linked to each other by many common features of landscape and human and cultural peculiarities. These, together with a shared past and similar experiences, account for the many surviving bonds between the peoples of this region, and the continued existence of these bonds is spontaneously and often unexpectedly revealed, especially in times of crisis.

For many centuries Vienna was the cultural, intellectual and political centre of the Danube region. In this role she continues to represent a powerful magnet for the population of the region. Thanks to our efforts to develop Vienna into an international centre we are now able to restore this central role to our federal capital, though under different conditions.

Unlike the United States or other political structures striving for national unity, the Austro-Hungarian monarchy, which governed the destiny of this region for centuries, was never a 'melting pot'. The nations within the monarchy led their own lives in many respects, not only practising their own languages and indigenous cultures but enjoying a measure of independence in many other spheres. Modern Austria is the smallest of the successor states of the monarchy, but she is the only one to practise western-type democracy. She has achieved a relatively high standard of living – the fruits of diligence and hard work – though admittedly this was achieved only after a great deal of suffering and hardship, many doubts about her viability and a number of reverses.

In the time of the monarchy the Danube region was a permanent centre of unrest: apart from being the bone of contention fought over by the great powers of the day, it was also exposed to recurrent upheavals brought by the rising tide of nationalism. Even after the First World War the successor states – and the Austrian republic was no exception – continued to be the real problem children of international politics because of continuous fluctuations in their political and economic development.

AUSTRIA AS A STABILIZING FACTOR

In contrast to this turbulent past, the Austria of the Second Republic has become a genuine stabilizing factor in the Danube region. She still has a role to play here, even though she is no longer a great power but merely an alpine republic with a population of seven million. Since we recovered full independence one of the main aims of our foreign policy, after the ups and downs of the period between the two wars and the immediate postwar period, has been to normalize our relations with the countries of Eastern Europe and to put them on an amicable basis. This was no easy task, since the consequences of East–West tension and of the cold war had a detrimental effect on Austria's relations with these countries. At that time there was virtually no question of a policy of peaceful coexistence; conflicting ideologies were at loggerheads and produced an international climate of mistrust that permitted scarcely any *rapprochement* between states with different ideological systems. Added to this was the fact that the unsolved problem of the Austrian state treaty was giving rise to uncertainty among the successor states of the former monarchy about Austria's future position in the international balance of power. Her attempts were being closely watched in the East European countries with some mistrust: the trauma of another *Anschluss* was a difficult one to shake off. An additional factor was the question of property, in particular of Austrian property in the East-bloc states; this was not merely a question of principle for it concerned extensive possessions that had formerly belonged to Austrian citizens who had left those countries either compulsorily or voluntarily.

The turning-point did not come until signing of the state treaty in 1955. This created the conditions for a readjustment of relations with the East European countries, but of course it took many years for the atmosphere of mistrust, which was characterized by continuous border incidents and mutual polemics, to give way to a policy of peaceful coexistence. It can be stated unreservedly that all Austrian governments since the rebirth of the Second Republic, and particularly since we attained full sovereignty in 1955, have constantly striven to normalize relations with the East-bloc states and to put them on a friendly basis. At first these efforts made but slight progress, but soon they found support both in the policy of peaceful coexistence inaugurated by Khrushchev and in the efforts of the western powers to achieve a *détente* in East–West relations. Even though these efforts suffered several serious setbacks – we need only recall the incident of the shooting down of the American U-2 reconnaissance aircraft over Soviet territory, or the crises over Cuba, Hungary and Czechoslovakia – it did eventually prove possible to uphold the idea of normalization of East–West relations and to intensify East–West contacts in the most varied spheres, especially in the non-political ones. This policy was repeatedly subjected to severe criticism from both sides. A great number of arguments were put forward to frustrate these efforts, the main ones being the security interests of one power group or the other. It is to the credit of the political skill and sobriety shown on both sides that in spite of objections and fierce recriminations the road of East–West understanding that we had chosen continued to be pursued and was indeed greatly extended.

It would be naive to shut our eyes to the German problem when we consider this development; there can surely be no doubt that this is the problem that has put a great strain on developments throughout Europe since the end of the Second

F

World War. We cannot overlook the fact that anxiety about German rearmament, with all the consequences this might entail, continues to exist in the eastern bloc. The Federal Republic of Germany is already the dominant partner in the European Economic Community and one day – this is the fear in the East – might again play a dominant part in the western community of states. This explains the persistent efforts by Moscow and the East European states to sign a treaty with Germany that would freeze the *status quo*, or in other words recognize the existing frontiers. It is in this light that Moscow's efforts to sign a non-aggression treaty with the Federal Republic of Germany must be seen.

AUSTRIA AND EUROPEAN SECURITY

European security, which is closely linked to these efforts, is one of the eastern bloc's main foreign policy problems. Hence its insistent call for a European security conference and for the setting up of a European security system. In the many talks that I have been able to have with East-bloc politicians in recent years these considerations emerged time and again – and invariably culminated in the demand for recognition of the *status quo*, i.e. of the existing frontiers in Europe. Thus the signing of a treaty with the Federal Republic of Germany renouncing the use of force undoubtedly represents a first and very vital step in this direction, especially as it expressly acknowledges the Oder–Neisse line and the border between the two German states. We have no space here to examine the domestic repercussions of this treaty in the Federal Republic of Germany and in the German Democratic Republic – but it can be stated that this treaty represents a further contribution to the *détente* between Eastern and Western Europe.

As a small neutral country at the intersection of the two great ideological and power-political groupings of our era, Austria clearly has a vital interest in the continuance and intensification of a policy of *détente*. Only in a politically relaxed atmosphere can a small neutral state in Austria's geopolitical situation develop fruitfully. This consideration underlies her positive attitude to a European security conference. Needless to say, it is in her own interest to respect existing frontiers.

Austria's relations with the East European states must therefore be seen against this development. Notwithstanding various setbacks she has managed since the signing of the state treaty continually to improve her relations with Eastern Europe, and has finally established them at a level that corresponds to the centuries-old tradition of relations between the nations of the Danube region. Let us not forget the numerous human ties that still exist today, so many decades after the collapse of the old empire, between the Austrians and their neighbours. Added to this are her numerous cultural and economic contacts with these countries. Many of her industries are traditionally oriented towards the East European market and therefore have an interest both in maintaining these relations and in developing them further. Attempts of this kind have been successful in recent years in spite of the differences in the various social systems.

As for the difficult question of compensation for confiscated Austrian property within the East European states, this has been solved in most cases by compromise. For the sake of a peaceful development of relations Austria has made considerable concessions in this field. She is convinced that by doing so she has made a major contribution not only to the settlement of this particular question but also to the peaceful development of relations generally. Only with her northern neighbour has she failed so far to solve this delicate question, important though it is to mutual relations. She has tried to achieve a settlement ever since the signing of the state treaty, and she has declared her willingness to make concessions, but these would of course have to be kept within a scale that the country – or rather the Austrian citizens concerned – could be reasonably expected to afford. The experience of the past few years shows that mutual recriminations and polemics cannot solve this problem but only aggravate it. It seems to me that one of the most important tasks of Austria's eastern policy in the immediate future is to find a satisfactory settlement by means of good sense and concessions on both sides.

It may be noted with satisfaction today that Austria's relations with the East European countries, despite a few temporary setbacks, have continued to develop in a favourable direction ever since the state treaty was signed. This is partly the result of a general policy of *détente* between East and West and partly – and this may be the decisive factor – due to consistent efforts on both sides to remove any mistrust surviving from the past and to achieve genuine understanding. Modern Austria no longer represents to the successor states the danger that she was still – surely wrongly – alleged to represent as recently as between the wars. Austrian foreign policy has succeeded in establishing confidence and in proving convincingly that she seeks nothing other than genuine good-neighbourly relations with all states, not least with those of Eastern Europe.

11

AUSTRIA AND THE UNITED NATIONS

The 1955 treaty and the declaration of Austria's permanent neutrality were the foundation-stones of Austria's foreign policy.

The year 1955, a highly important year for Austria, also saw the fulfilment of another long-cherished hope – on 14 December she was admitted to the United Nations. Nearly ten years had passed since she first applied for admission to this international organization, yet throughout all the years when admission seemed to have been shelved indefinitely she never surrendered her claim to a place in this community of states. She knew that the day would come; that was why she did not stand aloof, waiting for admission to the UN, but began to take an active part in several of its specialized agencies. The younger generation of Austrians was informed about the aims of the United Nations and the Austrian people as a whole understood the important part played by this world organization in the maintenance of peace. Thus the idea of the United Nations has always remained alive in Austria.

With her attainment of independence and her admission to the United Nations, Austria was once more able, after nearly twenty years of isolation, to assert her views in a world forum and collaborate in realizing the plans of the community of nations.

During the long years of occupation that Austria had to suffer we had come to the conclusion that the attainment of full sovereignty was possible only as part of a general international *détente*. This led us to embrace two maxims that have remained decisive for Austria's foreign policy to this day – permanent neutrality and the need to fix this principle firmly in the minds of all countries by our active participation in international communities – in other words, neutrality with a simultaneous belief in active international co-operation on the basis of the United Nations charter.

Admission to the UN represented a turning-point in the postwar history of Austria and became a vital, decisive element in her foreign policy. Similarly, the country's first public appearance in the world forum in 1956 emphasized the role that she intended to play in the United Nations as a neutral state and indeed is still playing to this day. That the right line was adopted in 1956 is proved by the fact that in her fourteen years of membership of the United Nations Austria has won an excellent position for herself. In spite of her small size she is one of the most highly respected member states, chiefly because she has succeeded in adopting a clear attitude in the international interplay of forces, an attitude that is highly appreciated, especially among the states recently admitted to the community. The eyes of the United Nations are nowadays frequently turned on Austria because it is well known that she is not one of those countries who take their decisions in accordance with the power grouping they belong to, but takes them solely on the strength of her own judgement. This objective and businesslike attitude of Austria's is much appreciated in the UN and has greatly reinforced her position in the world organization. It hardly needs stressing that – in view of Austria's international status – our situation is not always easy and that it requires thorough familiarity with the issues concerned and a simultaneous understanding of the trends in international politics.

In contrast to other medium and small countries who belong to systems of alliances and are able to follow the line of their treaty partners or consult with them in doubtful cases, Austria must make her decisions on her own. This is all the more difficult because a neutral state such as Austria has to make sure that the community of states remains confident in the objectivity and consistency of her policy. I mention this point because it is frequently thought that a neutral usually keeps out of difficult problems and avoids adopting a clear and unambiguous line. Since her admission to the United Nations Austria has never shrunk from formulating her convictions clearly and soberly. It can be stated with satisfaction that this objectivity is recognized and respected by the community of nations.

AUSTRIA'S ACTIVITY IN THE UNITED NATIONS

The esteem that Austria is enjoying in the United Nations is revealed among other things by the election of Austrian delegates to a number of important bodies within the world organization. The establishment in Vienna of the International Atomic Energy Agency (IAEA) and the Industrial Development Organization (Unido) laid the foundation for the setting up of a second UN centre in Europe – following the initial one in Geneva. The Austrian capital has thus increasingly become the venue for international meetings, as is testified by the numerous international conferences held in Vienna. For instance the big UN conferences on diplomatic and consular privileges and the first international state conference were all held there.

Austria's work in the United Nations began under difficult conditions – but she soon continued and intensified these activities by her efforts to help realize the principles embodied in the charter, in particular in the humanitarian field, in the sphere of peace-keeping and putting an end to the arms race, and finally in the important sector of aid to the distressed nations of the world. Over the past few years Austria has taken an active part along these lines in the discussion of numerous international problems, such as the disarmament talks, the work of the space agency (of which she is chairman) and the efforts to regulate the financial crisis of the United Nations, which is an extremely serious political issue. Finally she was for many years a member of the United Nations Economic and Social Council, the vital body of the world organization dealing with all social, humanitarian and economic questions.

It was because of Austria's policy of active participation in international affairs and her desire to contribute to the maintenance of peace that the federal government decided to answer the United Nations appeal and take part in the organization's peace-keeping operations in the Congo, in Cyprus and, within the framework of the organization supervising the armistice, in the Middle East. The use of Austrian medical contingents in the Congo has won Austria many friends not only in the United

Nations but also among the Congolese people. Much the same is true of the use of an Austrian policing contingent and medical unit in Cyprus over the past few years. By this action she has once more shown evidence of her faith in international co-operation for the peaceful settlement of disputes and has helped to protect this Mediterranean island from the horrors of civil war.

The law passed by the Austrian parliament in 1965 to regulate the participation of Austrian units in aid operations mounted by international organizations provided a most valuable basis for Austria's further participation in United Nations peace-keeping activities. Following the renewed outbreak of the Middle East conflict she did not hesitate to support its peace-keeping activity by supplying officers for the UN observer team on the Suez Canal.

In addition to co-operating in the political and economic work of the United Nations, Austria has also played a major part over the past few years in all the organization's activities in the humanitarian and human rights sector. She has for many years been a member of the UN Human Rights Commission and of the Committee for the Protection of Minorities, to which she attaches particular importance.

Whereas it is of no particular importance to a great power to ensure that the world organization will support it in preserving its national interests or defending its independence and sovereignty, this aspect is very important for a small country. A major power can defend its security and its national interests on its own if they are threatened by a third party, but a small country can do this on only a very limited scale. Timely help from an international community and in particular the existence of a forum to which the small country can if necessary turn when threatened to defend its rights or obtain aid in critical situations are therefore of vital importance. This has been repeatedly shown in the past, and many a critical situation has been ironed out by the intervention of the world organization or at least influenced to such an extent that it was easier to open negotiations to settle the conflict.

Quite apart from the United Nations' work in preventing entirely desirable by-product of this type of economic initiative.

Another problem that is always being pointed out by Austrian experts on foreign trade policy was discussed on the spot by our The fact that the United Nations offers the possibility of regular personal contact between the statesmen of our globe contributes greatly to a better understanding of the problems of member states. In the General Assembly, which meets annually, the nations of the world have also created a platform on which a dialogue between nations, between regions and between individuals has been made uniquely possible. I should like to refer here to a remark by Martin Buber, who said in 1952: 'Direct and frank dialogue is getting rarer and more difficult; more and more mercilessly the gulfs between people threaten to become unbridgeable. This is the fateful question that faces humanity. The future of man as man depends on the rebirth of the dialogue.' In the General Assembly all nations enjoy the privilege of equality, for there is no discrimination between races and different treatment is not meted out to countries on the basis of their territorial or numerical size. The United Nations charter wants all states to be heard on an equal basis. The importance of the United Nations becomes obvious here.

For Austria, too, the importance of these regular yearly contacts with the representatives of the other member states should not be underrated. Such contacts provide a clearer picture than anything else of the trends and views prevailing in the most varied parts of the world and these cannot be better observed or studied anywhere than in the United Nations. Thanks to the giant strides made by technology the world has become smaller, so no country today can be content to live in splendid isolation. Living contact with the world outside has become more necessary than ever if the correct decisions are to be made at the right moment. Austria's membership of the United Nations makes this kind of contact possible and therefore is of great help to Austria's foreign policy.

In this way Austria has managed to shake off the isolation into which she had been thrust by the tragic events of 1938 and their consequences, and to regain her rightful position on the world scene in view of her noble past and present achievements.

In a world of conflicts even an organization such as the United Nations cannot be free from problems. No one will deny that it has not been able to live up to the possibly over-bold hopes placed in it when it was founded. But it is only fair to say that it has been of incalculable value to international political progress over the last few decades: it has kept the dialogue between East and West going; it has shown a great many new Afro-Asian states the way into the community of nations; and last but not least it represents the world's conscience on the basis of the charter. It has thus become an irreplaceable moral force in the constellation of forces in international politics. In spite of the new crises that confront it and are threatening to drag it down to one of the lowest points in its history, the member states do seem to be moving towards the realization of what Dag Hammarskjöld once so strikingly formulated: 'We should recognize the United Nations for what it is – an admittedly imperfect but indispensable instrument for the nations, designed to ensure a more just and secure world order through peaceful evolution.'

12

ECONOMIC AID TO THE DEVELOPING COUNTRIES

Economic relations between the industrialized countries since the Second World War have been marked by their efforts to make their economies increasingly interdependent and steadily to extend trade between them. In doing so their aim is to promote economic growth and most of all to improve the population's standard of living by means of a rational international division of labour. Political stability and peaceful international relations were to be an additional bonus of such efforts.

In retrospect it can certainly be said that by and large these efforts have been successful and that their objectives have been reached. The instruments that the industrial states used in these attempts were a series of international agreements such as the General Agreement on Tariffs and Trade (Gatt) the Organization for European Economic Co-operation (OEEC), the Council for Mutual Economic Aid (Comecon) and finally the European Economic Community (EEC) and the European Free Trade Association (Efta). The work of these organizations has very largely determined the trade and foreign policy of the participating countries over the past twenty-five years. The very nature of the economic aims pursued meant of course that they were never fully achieved. The optimization of industrial and agricultural production processes, the maximization of productivity and the further intensification of foreign trade by means of a sensible division of labour between the various economies are requirements that still face our industrial countries. This will remain true in the future as well. The years to come will be characterized by co-operation between the industrialized countries in the economic sphere, with a view to improving the general prosperity of their people. This can be judged by the example of European integration to which Austria, too, attaches considerable importance. It is even possible that the political destiny of our continent may depend on whether we succeed in bringing the economies of the countries of Europe still closer together.

The destiny of the world, on the other hand, does not depend mainly on whether we hasten European integration. Over the last twenty years a different and more pressing problem has moved to the foreground, one that cannot be settled by a dialogue between the EEC and Efta, between Eastern and Western Europe, or between North America and Europe. This is the problem of how to bridge the economic gap between North and South, i.e. between the industrialized and the developing countries, between economies enjoying surpluses and those that encounter the greatest difficulties in satisfying even the most basic needs. This is a problem that we shall have to live with during the rest of the twentieth century. The industrialized countries will not be able to fulfil any of their responsibilities in the field of foreign or economic policy unless they bear in mind the urgent problem of economic aid to the developing countries.

GENERAL PROBLEMS

These facts were recently brought to the world's attention in a particularly emphatic way. An important part was played here by the UN General Assembly of 24 October 1970 when the 'second United Nations decade' was proclaimed in the presence of the heads of state and premiers of the member states, and by the publication of a series of fundamental and innovatory investigations into the problem of the development of the world's backward regions, such as the Pearson Report,[1] the Tinbergen Report,[2] the Peterson Report[3] and the Jackson Report.[4] It is to be hoped that the worldwide discussion and attention triggered off by these initiatives will not die down for a long time to come. It is already clear that the conclusions and recommendations contained in them will have – and indeed *must* have – a decisive effect on future policy for aid if economic and political relations between the countries of our globe are to develop in a way that will serve universal peace.

This should be made easier by the fact that although the experts who prepared these reports embarked from differing stand-points, they largely arrived at the same results, which proves that the problem of aid can be viewed entirely objectively. This comes as something of a surprise, since a quick glance at the most recent past will reveal considerable differences in the origin, the political and social structure, the economic conditions and the socio-political aspirations of the hundred-odd developing states in the world. The task of assessing actual conditions and possible lines of development on a qualitative basis and the quantification of the data are both highly complex tasks. The differences between the developing countries are often enormous. On the one hand there are states that can best be described as sub-continents, such as India, while others are very small in area. Much the same applies to population figures. There are also differences in climate and availability of raw materials and these make it difficult, if not impossible, to work out common criteria.

But whatever the difficulties involved in working out a unified aid policy and in implementing it in a way that will benefit both the developing and the industrialized countries, behind all these efforts there is a fundamental and positive belief in the efficacy of this kind of international solidarity; according to the Pearson Report, this solidarity is essentially of a moral nature: 'It is only right that the wealthy should share their wealth with the poor.'[5] It is gratifying that this ethical motivation behind solidarity in economic and social matters, which not so long ago would certainly not have been a matter of course even among people in the same country, has now entered the relations between nations.

I shall deal with Austria's attitude to aid to the developing countries in greater detail later in this chapter, but I should like to emphasize here that precisely this kind of moral motivation was the most important factor behind the Austrian government's efforts in this field in recent years. The Austrian's tendency to help strangers and to live in friendship with them – a characteristic that stems from our nation's history and the position of our state – backed up the government in a decisive way. Not only in Austria but in all industrialized countries the government must be able to rely on ordinary people seeing aid to the developing countries as a moral duty and on their being willing to make certain sacrifices for it.

This will be easier when it is more clearly realized in the donor countries that aid can yield very concrete advantages, even if these cannot always be taken up at once. These advantages need not be economic, for the setting up or deepening of friendly relations, accompanied by a respect for sovereignty on both sides, may represent a highly desirable longer-term objective of aid.

Any aid that is bound up with the hope of exerting a political influence on the receiver country, or even making it dependent, is incompatible with the moral motivation we have spoken of and is unlikely ever to achieve the desired objective, or at least not on any permanent basis.

What then can the developing countries, which at present account for about two-thirds of the world's population, really expect from aid? What is the point of the rich giving away some of their wealth?

It is essentially a case of enabling the poorer countries to catch up with the industrial and technological progress of our age and thus increase the prosperity of their peoples. Nobody believes that this can be done in a hurry or that it will be possible to eliminate all differences in income and abolish all inequalities. The point is that these differences should be suitably mitigated and fair opportunities should be provided for the economic advancement both of individuals and of the developing countries as a whole.

The question then arises as to whether the chances of reaching this objective in the long run are good. To answer this we can usefully draw on such experience as has already been accumulated in this field.

An assessment of experiences made over the past twenty years produces some encouraging results.[6] The average growth-rate of the gross national product of the developing countries was about 5 per cent annually from 1960 to 1967, whereas that of the industrialized countries was 4.8 per cent over the same period. It is true that this growth did not lead to a growth in *per capita* income in the developing countries, since their large population increase mopped up half the growth-rate. But a comparison with the growth-rates at earlier stages in the development of the industrialized countries shows that a 2.5 per cent growth-rate in *per capita* income is appreciable and an encouraging sign for the developing countries.

This overall statement of the case[7] should not blind us to the fact that developments in the past – and this presumably also applies to the future – vary a great deal from one developing country to another and from one region to another. In spite of the favourable conclusions reached by the experts about the sucesses in international development work since the Second World War, care will have to be taken to ensure that as far as possible all the developing countries benefit equally from it. Otherwise we should run the risk of intensifying or even perpetuating a disparity in economic development among the poorer countries while reducing the disparities between the industrialized countries and the more advanced developing countries.

As for the means and measures to be applied by the industrialized countries so as to achieve the objectives of successful aid, there is generally speaking a great measure of agreement among the experts. They call first for the export revenue of the developing countries to be raised, but this of course presupposes that they produce sufficient quantities of exportable goods, and at prices that are internationally competitive. But price alone is not the decisive factor in assessing the sales prospects of the developing countries. The success of the export policy for the developing countries depends very largely on the trade policy, or in other words on the foreign trade system that the economically developed partner applies to the exporting developing country. As a result, over the past few years questions of general trade policy have become as important as the concept of direct financial aid. Two points should be particularly noted in this connection – firstly an improvement of world market prices for primary materials, and secondly the introduction of a preferential tariff for manufactured and semi-manufactured goods from developing countries.

The stabilization of world market prices for primary products from the developing countries and where possible a raising of prices for certain other manufactured goods are objectives that more than any other form of aid would assure the developing countries of a revenue untainted by the stain of charity. It is regrettable that no decisive progress has yet been made in this field and that not all the international market organizations originally envisaged have yet been set up. In the European countries in particular there is a feeling that such market organ-

izations are an important prerequisite for the improvement and
stabilization of the export earnings of developing countries. Such
arrangements have already been made for coffee[8], tin[9] and even for
wheat, olive oil and sugar; they have confirmed in a most encouraging way that the objective aimed at is fully attainable. An
agreement on cocoa is to be expected shortly. This procedure is
clearly not possible for all products in which developing countries
have strong export interests – but the spirit of joint responsibility being held by the exporting and importing countries
demands that a pragmatic policy should be followed even in
difficult cases.

The importance attached to such arrangements by the
developing countries was brought home to me by talks I had in
connection with the visit of an Austrian goodwill mission to
Africa in the autumn of 1970. In all contacts with African spokes-
men the emphasis was on the need to grant the developing
countries more stable world market prices for agricultural products. As for the introduction of preferential tariffs for
manufactured and semi-manufactured goods from the developing
countries, this is particularly necessary because it should encourage industrialization. The creation of international market organizations to keep raw material prices pegged high would not in itself
serve this objective. It is true that manufactured and semi-manufactured goods at present account for only a small proportion of
exports from the developing countries; but this should make it
easier for the industrial countries to demonstrate their desire for
co-operation. Any such preferential ruling, as drafted by the UN
World Trade Conference and by the OECD and now under discussion there, must of course be adjusted to the differing potentials
of the industrialized countries and also to the differences in the
existing industrial structures of the developing countries. Generally speaking, however, only the abolition of tariffs by the industrial countries can in the long run ensure that the industrial sector
will also make its contribution to the progressive growth of the
developing countries.

No doubt the large European market that is now emerging will
have to pay particular attention to these problems. Quite apart
from a general regulation such as that now being discussed within
Unctad and the OECD, there are many opportunities left for the
industrial countries to make import concessions to the developing

countries. The waiver of tax burdens on specific manufactures (coffee and tea etc.) is, in Austria's experience, an example worth quoting here.

There is of course no doubt – even though theoretical economists are not entirely agreed on this point – that the granting of trade concessions to the developing countries cannot easily be bracketed with the demand for full reciprocity in free trade. After the Second World War this principle did admittedly prove decisive for the recovery of the industrial nations, and its complete realization will continue to be the object of our foreign trade policy for the next few years – but in relations between developed and developing countries it cannot be applied for the time being. In the interests of a suitable and sensible policy of industrialization the developing countries will have to look for sympathetic understanding for their demand that they must be allowed to practise an import policy that is to a certain extent protectionist.

This principle has already been widely accepted on a regional basis, as is shown by the agreement reached (or extended) in Yaounde between the European Economic Community and its seventeen associated African countries plus Madagascar. Like the EEC agreement with the East African states of Kenya, Tanzania and Uganda (the Arusha Agreement) and the agreement between the EEC and Nigeria (the Lagos Agreement), this provides for a free-trade zone within which the developing countries are granted free access to the Common Market, while the EEC receives tariff concessions in the markets of its associates for a limited number of goods only. This system has clearly proved successful – in spite of criticism – since the South American countries are now showing interest in a similar arrangement with the EEC.

It should be pointed out here that trade policy is more than an instrument for implementing an aid policy in relations between the industrial and developing countries; it can and should be applied in relations between one developing country and another in order to stimulate trade between them. The industrial countries should therefore show understanding for initiatives aimed at effecting preferential trade arrangements between the various developing countries, as has already been done successfully both in Africa (the Central African Market) and in South America (the Andes Pact).

But the economic development of the third world is not only fostered by the granting of trade concessions for raising the export earnings of the developing countries; the same objective is achieved by the direct encouragement of industry in the developing countries, which both improves their competitive position and diminishes their dependence on imports.

This requires an increased flow of capital into the developing countries. The past record of the industrialized countries in this respect is certainly respectable: in 1968 their net financial provisions amounted to no less than 12,858 million dollars, of which 11,699 million were provided by members of the Development Aid Committee (DAC) of the OECD alone;[10] this represents 0.97 per cent of the national revenue or 0.77 per cent of the gross national product of the DAC members.[11] Most of this financial aid came from public funds and there is good reason to hope that these sums will again be increased, despite an undeniable degree of stagnation. This will be chiefly because the donor countries are genuinely trying to implement a recommendation voted by the second world trade and development conference of the United Nations in New Delhi in 1968; this proposed that each advanced country should try to make available to the developing countries a net annual amount representing at least 1 per cent of its gross national product at market prices. So far this recommendation has been implemented by only a few of the industrialized countries, chiefly those with traditional overseas interests, such as France, Belgium, the Netherlands and Britain, but – and this is worth noting – also by Switzerland and the Federal Republic of Germany. We shall come back to Austria's contribution later.

It is generally acknowledged that what matters to the developing countries is not merely the amount of financial aid; more important are the relevant conditions, in particular whether the inflow is predominantly of public rather than private capital and whether the terms – the Pearson Report speaks in this connection of 'soft' terms[12] – can therefore be made more advantageous to the developing countries. The expected additional aid from donor countries is likely to depend on evidence being produced that more effective use is being made of such finance.

Trade preferences and financial facilities as instruments of aid have been most effectively applied where there has been both a readiness and the necessary conditions on the part of the recipient country to mobilize its own forces on behalf of economic development. It appears that these prerequisites and national efforts can be greatly intensified in the developing countries by the provision of technical aid. Experts and aid officials are a very vital adjunct to the trade and financial contributions of the industrialized states since they make it possible, for relatively little outlay, to transmit technological know-how and therefore – more than any other form of aid – crystallize self-help in the developing countries. In this area we are still only just beginning to understand all the possibilities. It is particularly gratifying to Austria that she is the host country of Unido, the special organization of the United Nations concerned with encouraging aid on a multilateral basis; its efforts have so far been largely responsible for the fact that the scale of such aid throughout the world has increased more over the past few years than any other form of aid.

This brings me to a demand that has increasingly been voiced in recent years and is also repeatedly made in the expert report; this involves strengthening the multilateral development aid system in which the international organizations concerned with fostering aid would be in a position to play a leading part and to make aid a genuinely international community programme.[13]

These considerations certainly deserve our attention, for there is nothing that implements the idea of international solidarity as manifested in aid to developing countries quite so much as concentrating the efforts of both sides in multilateral organizations. Particularly for smaller countries such as Austria with limited means, this opens up better possibilities for making a more effective contribution to aid. But these organizations can fulfil these tasks only if they constantly assess their work and their expenditure according to results. This is a matter that should concern the recipient countries as well as the donor countries. Besides, it is the only way to ensure general understanding for the transfer to the international organizations of greater responsibility for economic aid.

Whether our community of states can meet the challenge with which it is now so urgently faced and which demands from it a vast amount of determination and an equal amount of unselfishness will depend on whether these tasks are tackled. Are we really going to fail and miss this unique opportunity of making a decisive contribution to the preservation of peace in our time through global solidarity in the economic field?

AUSTRIA'S CONTRIBUTIONS

As I have already indicated, Austria has taken up this challenge and has repeatedly stated that she is willing to make increased efforts, together with the other industrialized countries, to co-operate with the nations of the third world in the coming decade, which has been labelled by the United Nations the 'second development decade'. In the OECD Council of Ministers Austria stated that she would support the efforts of the United Nations and its specialist organizations in this direction, that she would step up her development aid as far as possible and that she would endeavour, by concentrating her efforts, to provide the maximum aid.[14]

The contributions made by Austria over the past few years, especially her public and private contributions to economic aid for the developing countries, have shown that these were no empty words. In 1969 these amounted to 80.7 million dollars nett as against 73.7 in 1968 (plus 10 per cent). In 1967 the figure was only 47.9 million dollars. Austria's net financial contributions within the framework of aid to the developing countries therefore increased by 70 per cent from 1967 to 1969. This represented, in 1969, 0.87 per cent of Austria's social product and 0.65 per cent of her gross national product; in 1967 the respective percentages had been only 0.6 and 0.36. The average figure for all OECD/DAC countries in 1968 was 0.97 per cent of the social product and 0.77 per cent of the gross national product.

Of Austria's net financial contribution of 80.7 million dollars 22.3 million dollars or 27.6 per cent were made up of public contributions, and 58.4 million dollars or 72.4 per cent by private contributions; 15.4 million dollars or 19 per cent were supplied through multilateral channels. These were mainly direct contributions to international organizations and long-term loans to such organizations. This means that within two years Austria's multilateral aid had doubled from the 1967 figure of only 7.6 million dollars. In this way she has emphasized the special importance she attaches to multilateral aid and her support of an international tendency – on the part of both the donor country and the recipient country – to make economic aid more multilateral. Austria welcomes this development, if only because it relieves her of the need to set up an extensive administrative apparatus to manage her aid. The same administrative advantages are also enjoyed by the developing countries, whose authorities can work more effectively with international organizations rather than struggling laboriously through a tangle of national projects and tenders in which it is easy to lose one's way. With her relatively large share in multilateral aid to the developing countries Austria occupies a top place in overall aid among all OECD/DAC countries.

Austria's private contributions – assessed by the OECD/DAC as aid in the narrower sense – amounted in 1969 to 58.4 million dollars or 72.4 per cent of all aid. These were state-guaranteed export credits, or private financing and export credits, bilateral direct investments, long-term contributions and so on. This represented an increase of 12.5 per cent compared to 1968, when these contributions reached a total of 46.8 million dollars. An above-average growth-rate was shown chiefly by direct investments.

But to appreciate the full extent of the economic aid provided by Austria to the developing countries over the last few years we must not merely count the expenditure that has in the past been described and accepted as aid of this kind by the relevant international bodies. There is a number of additional forms of expenditure that have not so far been internationally acknowledged to constitute aid. They include, for instance, the money spent by Austria to enable students from the developing countries to attend her educational establishments. In 1967 this amounted to no less than 4.3 million dollars. To this must be added expenditure on the residential and teaching premises used by these students – a further 0.7 million dollars. The same is true of Austria's waiver of customs revenue from the imports of certain products from the developing countries, such as tropical foodstuffs, spices, tobacco and so on. This loss of revenue, which represents genuine aid to the developing countries, amounted to

more than 12 million dollars in 1969, according to the calcula-
tions of the Austrian finance authorities. If we add to this the
sums spent on technical aid by private organizations in Austria,
to the tune of 4.2 million dollars, then her overall economic aid
to the developing countries amounted to 101.9 million dollars in
1969. This represents 1.1 per cent of her total product and 0.82
per cent of her gross national product.

Austria is thus going the right way about realizing the target
set by the community of industrialized countries; this stated
that aid during the 'second development decade' (1971–80)
should amount to 1 per cent of each country's gross national
product. It is expected that the drafting of a medium-term aid
plan by the Austrian federal government will result in a further
concentration of all resources and thus make it possible for
Austria to increase her contribution. This of course applies both
to direct financial aid and to the technical aid that Austria supplies
from public funds.

Needless to say, Austria gives preference to the areas in which
she possesses particular know-how and expertise. These are
chiefly projects designed to solve general educational and school-
ing problems, the planning of tourist traffic, projects in certain
areas of agriculture and forestry and in industry. In the industrial sector the projects are mainly concerned with building
power stations and power grids, bridges and residential accommodation, and, last but not least, with regional planning.

There is admittedly a tendency in Austria to concentrate
technical aid geographically, her attention being mainly focused
on the Mediterranean area and the Middle East, as well as on a
few key areas in Asia. She is always trying to move her training
programmes in the field of technological aid into the developing
countries themselves. This tendency is reflected in the fact that
at present only 20 per cent of all technological aid expenditure is
spent actually in Austria.

As an alternative to multilateral and bilateral aid Austria has in
recent years attempted to use her resources even more effectively by providing her aid jointly with other industrialized
countries. This objective was served, among other things, by the
agreement she made with Switzerland on 23 August 1967 to co-
operate with her in the field of technological aid to the developing
countries. Experience so far suggests that this was a successful

idea; there has been a valuable exchange of information and concrete co-operation on individual projects; for example the two countries carried out one such joint project in Rwanda.

Although Austria is not properly speaking a capital-exporting country, and although the prospects are slight of her becoming one on any major scale in the immediate future, the appropriate Austrian authorities are nevertheless anxious to put the domestic capital market at the service of aid as well. The idea is mainly that the international organizations should be invited to place loans or parts of loans in Austria. Attempts in this direction have so far been entirely successful. Thus for instance the Inter-American Development Bank placed loans in Austria in 1968 and 1969 and the Asian Development Bank in 1970.

WORLDWIDE TRADE RELATIONS

This brief outline of the nature and scope of Austrian economic aid to the developing countries should not convey the impression that Austria's economic relations with the countries of the third world are to be viewed purely from this point of view. This is by no means the case. The scope of her economic relations with the developing countries is far greater and is certainly not confined to such aid, which after all is designed merely to enable the developing countries to stand on their own feet economically one day. This means that they must become partners with the present-day industrialized countries and not forever remain the recipients of charity – a position they themselves do not relish.

The strongest incentive everywhere is the development of trade between the industrialized and developing countries. For a country like Austria in particular, with (compared to the international average), a highly complex foreign trade pattern, this represents a challenge from which our export industry should not shy away. So far it seems that they still frequently do so, despite some isolated and localized successes by individual firms. Both the scale and the trend of our economic relations with the developing countries seem to confirm this.

While Austria's overall exports increased by 105.5 per cent between 1959 and 1969, the rate of increase of our exports to developing countries was a mere 50.4 per cent during the same period. The same picture is revealed by imports. Between 1958 and 1968 Austria's total imports increased by 118 per cent, but imports from the developing countries increased by only 87.5 per cent. Even when these figures are broken down by region the growth-rate of trade relations with the developing countries still lies far below those for Efta, the EEC or Comecon. This trend is particularly obvious if we look at the relative share of the developing countries in Austria's overall imports and exports. Their percentage share in her exports have dropped from 14.85 (1967) to 9.2 (1968). Imports reveal a similar picture: 8.78 in 1967 and 16.9 in 1968.[15]

On the import side this trend – admittedly one that can be seen in all the industrialized countries – may be due mainly to the lack of flexibility in Austria's demand for raw materials, which account for the majority of imports from the developing countries. In the export field, where manufactured and semi-manufactured goods predominate, it appears that we have lost certain positions in the developing countries. These were presumably neglected in favour of the encouraging and continuing boom in Europe. It is questionable whether these positions can be won back just as quickly when the need again arises, or whether greater and more strenuous efforts will be needed to recover them for the development of markets in Europe.[16]

It is only fair to admit that a number of Austrian firms, including of course the most important and efficient, have made considerable efforts to gain a foothold in the markets of the developing countries. Firms involved in the chemical industry, mechanical engineering and transport engineering have scored particular successes here. For some of them in fact exports to the developing countries play a far bigger part than might be suspected from Austria's overall import and export statistics.

It is therefore a matter of course that the Austrian authorities must do everything to support the efforts being made by individual firms. It is in this light that the goodwill mission that visited a number of African states in September 1970 should be seen. It was the first time that Austria had dispatched an official mission of this kind to Africa and thus demonstrated her interest in the continent. In all the countries they visited the members of the mission found that the Africans were willing to intensify their relations with Austria, especially their economic relations. The Africans time and again and spontaneously pointed to the fact – which was highly relevant to them – that Austria was widely trusted in Africa both as a permanently neutral state and because throughout her history she had never possessed any colonies. We were assured that Africans preferred to enter into economic relations with a country like ours than with a major country that was bound by treaties and whose colonial past and present political interests induced the developing countries to show a certain reserve. This friendly willingness – and it is also found outside Africa – to strengthen economic relations with Austria should be taken up in every possible way. Unfortunately there are still far too few Austrian diplomatic missions to the developing countries, with the result that they can barely look after the vast areas assigned to them. Much the same is true of the excellent trade delegates. It is probably an inescapable fact that in future Austrian official representatives will have to have their road prepared for them, at least temporarily, by the pioneering work of the representatives of Austrian business firms.

At any rate, the problem will not be solved by the sale of consumer goods alone. The example of other industrialized European countries shows that they concentrate mainly on the export of capital goods which, needless to say, yield a far larger revenue than the sale of consumer goods. As the developing countries are now at a stage of economic restructuring, so that a new start will have to be made in virtually every branch of the economy and industry, great opportunities are opening up for the Austrian capital goods industry; and as the goodwill mission proved, Austrian export interests are also profiting by the progressive consolidation of political conditions in Africa.

In view of the diminishing risks and considering Austria's potential for promoting exports to the developing countries both in terms of finance and in personnel, it really should be easy enough to develop her commercial presence overseas – which properly speaking dates only from the Second World War – in such a way that the lead of the other industrialized countries in this field is eliminated. The prospects are favourable. An increasing opening-up of relations with the rest of the world would be an entirely desirable by-product of this type of economic initiative.

Another problem that is always being pointed out by Austrian experts on foreign trade policy was discussed on the spot by our goodwill mission; this was the need to make our foreign trade statistics more informative in respect of trade with the developing countries. In the absence of any trade in raw materials of her own, Austria imports most of her raw materials from the developing countries not direct but in a roundabout way via commodity exchanges or commodity dealers in Western Europe. The result is that Austria's raw material imports do not appear at all, or only minimally, in the trade balance sheets of the developing countries. It took some explaining by the members of the Austrian mission in Africa to make the Africans realize the true extent of Austrian imports from Africa. This explanation was met with the request that Austria should in future make more purchases direct from Africa.

Without wishing to diminish the importance of the export of goods we should also discuss whether Austria's relations with the developing countries could not be complemented by more patent, licence or know-how agreements, or by participation arrangements.

I have already referred to the fundamental question of relations between the developing countries and the industrialized world. There can be no doubt that Austria's future will depend not only on the peaceful development of relations within the great power blocs of our age, in other words between East and West, but also very much on solving the problem of relations between the highly industrialized North and the underdeveloped South of our globe. Let us not indulge in illusions; only a satisfactory solution of this question, which will enable the developing countries to promote their economy freely and independently and thus to become true partners with the industrialized states, will save them from grave social conflict and us from the effects of such a development. The United Nations have contributed very substantially to the creation of a better understanding for these problems, but we must frankly admit that we are still a long way from solving them. In this process a useful part can be played by small neutral countries such as Austria. As we have seen, they enjoy the confidence of the developing countries because they have usually never possessed any overseas colonies and because they are not suspected of harbouring power-political aspirations. This is particularly true of neutral states, which is why the developing countries most frequently turn to them for advice and of course also for aid. As a poor country from the capital point of view we may still do a great deal of useful work in the advisory field, both with our goodwill and by making our know-how available.

One of the main reasons why western business firms are very reluctant to invest in the developing countries of Africa is that they are afraid of the effects of the lack of internal political stability. They frequently make critical references to the fact that the power struggles in Africa have not yet come to an end. To this we might reply that the period of uncertainty is now over and that nowadays orderly conditions prevail in most of the new African states. Moreover experience has shown that these countries scrupulously observe their obligations under economic and co-ordination agreements. It seems therefore desirable for the sake of both sides that the industrialized countries should seek economic co-operation with the developing countries on a larger scale than they have done so far.

Let me add one more word on the critical attitude I have just referred to. We must not forget that the nations of Europe fought each other fiercely for many centuries and that countless wars had to be waged before our continent eventually found its true character. How can we in fairness expect the African states, which won their independence only a few years ago, to avoid a process of development that we ourselves had to pass through? It is to be hoped that modern developments with their technological achievements will help facilitate this process, and it seems that the countries concerned are well on the way to solving their problems after the initial upheavals of their struggle for liberation. But the success of these efforts will depend largely on whether we are prepared to grant these states the economic and social aid they so urgently require. Let me repeat: the future both of the developing countries themselves and of all the other nations on this earth will depend on the success of this great undertaking.

13

A FOREIGN POLICY FOR AUSTRIA

More than any other aspect of its public life a country's foreign policy is exposed to critical examination. This is chiefly due to the fact that the background of foreign policy is not always fully known to those who are not directly concerned with it. The verdict of the public, and frequently of the mass media, is very often based on inadequate information or on bald government communiqués, so that the doors are thrown open wide to surmise and speculation, and frequently to incorrect conclusions. This is not meant as a reproach, but merely as an explanation of the fact that all over the world the foreign policy of one's own country, and of course also that of other states, is very often judged wrongly, or at least in a distorting light. This of course raises the question of why governments or foreign ministries do not make enough of the necessary information available. This is an issue that has come very much into the foreground in recent years, concerning as it does the relationship between the mass media and foreign policy generally. I should like to make a few observations on this subject.

FOREIGN POLICY AND THE MASS MEDIA

Our century has witnessed both progressive democratization and enormous development in the field of technology. The acceleration and extension of the transmission of news and of transport facilities has resulted in a revolutionary transformation of the opportunities available to the mass media as information channels. Because of this the most recent events in any country or continent, as well as the relations between states, are brought to the notice of the information consumer with such speed and in such detail that even foreign policy and international relations cannot fail to be strongly affected.

It is obvious that these circumstances must also have a perceptible effect on the working methods of foreign policy. We know that in contemporary society the importance of information in public life and of the press, radio and television as media for gathering, processing and disseminating information can scarcely be overrated. With the growing complexity of political life the citizen cannot form a proper opinion of public events and use his vote according to his own interests unless he has reliable information at his disposal. This means that in democratic states the individual has a positive right to information, and that conversely the democratic state has a duty to supply its people with the appropriate information.

At the same time, however, the political, economic and social interdependence of countries is increasing, so that the individual's interest in events is no longer confined to his own country but increasingly embraces world events.

In transmitting information the mass media exert a considerable influence on forming public opinion. According to the findings of modern mass psychology, this can lead to them being misused for propaganda purposes if governments or interested groups use them to distort objective facts, to circulate propaganda, to doctor news or even to turn it into the exact opposite of what it should be. Deliberate manipulation of the mass media represents a danger to the individual, a danger that must not be underrated, and it is up to all of us to do everything in our power to oppose such interference with the objective transmission of information.

The first man to make and support such a demand was an Englishman, Jeremy Bentham, who demanded in his *Principles of International Law*, written in 1787-8 but published posthumously in 1843, that freedom of the press should be granted universally and that secret diplomacy should be completely eliminated. The idea was to let public opinion sanction the implementation of the norms and rulings of international law and in this manner to guarantee peace among nations. Bentham's ideas were far ahead of his time. The freedom of the journalist, his right to criticize, and the citizen's right to express his opinion freely had to be painfully wrested from the authoritarian thinking of the old-time state, run as it was by officialdom and the military, before it began to be realized that these freedoms were not rooted somewhere beyond the state order but within the community of free men. A long and difficult road, with many setbacks, had to be travelled before it was realized that by granting these liberties the state helped to strengthen a democratic sense of responsibility in its citizens and in this way was itself strengthened.

Democracy is based upon the conflict of opinion and the mass media play a decisive part in the process of shaping opinions and attitudes. The term 'public opinion' is frequently used. But only in the rarest of instances does this result from new ideas developed independently by ordinary people. Far more often it requires an apparatus of the kind available only to organized groups or institutions, such as the mass media. 'Public opinion' therefore generally emerges in such a way that a view is formulated by groups whose aim is to form opinions and this view is then either accepted or rejected by the public. So public opinion need not always be genuine, or in other words shaped by the people themselves; far more often it is 'manufactured' by groups representing sectional interests. The creation of public opinion depends on many factors, and satisfactory results will be achieved only if the principle of publicity is always borne in mind and the legal guarantees in relation to opinion forming are jealously safeguarded.

In addition to the freedom of the press, Bentham also demanded the abolition of secret diplomacy. On this issue, too, he was ahead of his time. History has shown us now that politics in general and foreign politics in particular have become increasingly public over the past 100 to 150 years. After the end of the First World War secret diplomacy, which until then had played an overwhelming part in international relations, became well and truly taboo. Originally, however, secret diplomacy was not so much directed against a country's own population, which anyway was not then a contributory factor, as against her foreign partners in negotiations. It was thus regarded as entirely legitimate. Only when governments began to yield to the public demand for information on everything that was happening did the problem of keeping certain political aspects secret from one's own people arise.

In a modern democracy foreign policy has very largely become a public matter. Questions relating to foreign policy are discussed every day in the press, in parliament and at public meetings. Meetings between statesmen can no longer be kept secret and the results of such contacts can no longer be kept from the public. We know that such meetings, especially if they are multilateral – i.e. international conferences between states – are covered in such detail by the mass media that several hundred and occasionally more than a thousand press and radio representatives are present at the conference. This intensive coverage of events relating to foreign policy is to be welcomed in principle as being in line with the democratization of foreign policy, but on the other hand we cannot close our eyes to the fact that it often results in considerable pressure being exerted by public opinion upon the course of the negotiations. In certain circumstances, especially if the pressure is exerted from certain quarters, the result may be that problems become matters of prestige and that the latitude for compromise is dangerously restricted. In fact there have been repeated warnings that excessive publicity can jeopardize the success of negotiations.

This brings us back to the problem of secrecy. In principle I should say that this is particularly necessary in the military sphere, i.e. in the case of matters directly touching the state's external security and independence. But this restriction also applies, up to a certain point, to foreign policy matters; while secret diplomacy must be rejected on principle, a certain measure of reticence is necessary in certain circumstances. The extent of this reticence largely depends in a democracy on the confidence that the government enjoys with the public and the mass media.

This brings me to the heart of the matter – the relationship between politics, in particular foreign politics, and the public and the mass media. In democratic states the media can exert a very considerable influence on politics. I should like to quote here Professor Rudolf Blühdorn, the Austrian international lawyer, who has formulated the crux of the problem very clearly: 'Public opinion becomes significant in domestic and foreign policy when it reflects a spontaneous reaction to some event, some piece of news, or some government measure, a reaction so emphatically expressed that the government feels inclined to take notice of it.

In this way public opinion can contribute to the shaping of the political will in a state.'

The attention paid to public opinion – according to Professor Blühdorn – is due to the fact that a country's policy ultimately depends on the voluntary co-operation of the public. I believe that this view is now universally accepted. It is therefore necessary to create a climate of confidence for a government's policy. Both in domestic policy, where problems usually touch the individual citizen directly and therefore interest him, and in the field of foreign policy it would seem necessary to gain the public's understanding and participation by supplying continuous and detailed information on the objectives and tasks of this policy. Only a foreign policy supported by the consent of overwhelming sections of the population can be effective in the long run.

A further objective of foreign policy – and here it differs fundamentally from domestic policy – must be to create this type of confidence abroad as well. This involves an effort to create a positive image of the country and its population.

As for the business of reporting of international events, it should be remembered that only very few newspapers and only a limited number of radio or television stations are in a position today to support a worldwide network of correspondents. This means that most of the information media are dependent on the relatively small groups of big news agencies, with the result that these wield an enormous power over information. A handful of agencies, or rather their correspondents working at some spot on the globe, can convey to the rest of the world a picture of an event at that spot, and this picture becomes decisive in shaping their opinion. The state information machinery cannot compete with these worldwide agencies in speed or effectiveness. This does not mean that I wish to criticize the work of these 'upper ten' of the mass media; I merely want to emphasize the high degree of responsibility that attaches to this group in the shaping of opinion within the international sphere.

For all these reasons it is indispensable for the state to practise an active information policy. Information on foreign policy problems and measures, if it is really to achieve its purpose, must not be confined to sporadic evasive or defensive utterances, denials or corrections. Instead the public must be continuously, systematically and objectively informed about the government's foreign policy. This includes a steady supply of background information to leading representatives of the mass media to ensure a fuller understanding of the various acts of foreign policy. This of course presupposes the existence of a relationship of trust between politicians and diplomats on the one side and journalists on the other.

It has always been one of the tasks of a diplomat to observe, analyse and report on public opinion as reflected in reports and commentaries by the mass media in his host country and, whenever possible, to influence public opinion in favour of his own country. It is his task to inform and instruct the public of his host country at regular intervals about the general principles and objectives, special requirements, measures and actions of his own country's foreign policy. The worldwide integration of news and information has created unprecedented opportunities for the promotion of mutual understanding and international friendship. It is in this light that the changed relations between foreign policy and diplomacy on the one hand and the mass media on the other must be assessed, and this new relationship should offer the necessary directives for an effective information policy.

This changed view of the nature of information policy is nowadays labelled 'public relations'. I am here touching on a subject whose far-reaching importance in the field of foreign policy has not always been realized up to now. There have of course always been methods of publicity, but the systematic manner in which publicity is now practised, the integration of sociological insights and psychological experience, of opinion polling and marketing, have been developed into a kind of science only in recent years. The diplomat's 'public relations' work cannot be done at his desk but only by his cultivation of personal contacts with the leading political journalists and representatives of the mass media.

FOREIGN POLICY AND PERMANENT NEUTRALITY

The Austro-Hungarian monarchy, a great power which for many centuries had played its part in determining the destinies of Europe, collapsed in 1918. Unlike the United States and other countries, it had not represented a state system striving for national unity. The nations represented in the monarchy very

G

largely led their own lives; this was reflected in their own languages and cultures and in many other respects as well. Behind the image of the old Austria, distinguished by imperial splendour, with a large number of nations and a great power policy focused principally on the Danube region and south-eastern Europe, there was all of a sudden nothing more than a small country, the newly founded Austrian Republic – a state which during the first few decades of its existence did not seem able to achieve a fundamental reorientation of its international position. There was, moreover, a good deal of doubt, both at home and abroad, about the political and economic viability of the new state. Added to this was the fact that the last few years before 1938 had been overshadowed by an increasingly difficult defensive struggle against National Socialism. The year 1938 finally saw the end of Austria's sovereignty and hence also of an Austrian foreign policy.

After the Second World War it took ten years for Austria to regain her full freedom and the ability to conduct a foreign policy. The treaty signed in 1955 by Austria and the four great powers and the status of permanent neutrality decreed by the Austrian parliament after she had attained full independence have since formed the foundations of Austria's independence and sovereignty. Her view of foreign policy therefore follows inevitably from these two premises.

Ever since 1955 the main aim of Austria's policy in relation to other countries has been to keep alive, by means of a realistic and active foreign policy, the interest of the outside world and especially of the great powers in the maintenance of her independence and neutrality. After all, her external security depends not only on her strict observance of her own neutrality but also on the importance that the powers with interests in the region attach to the maintenance of this neutrality. We must therefore prove to other states that the existence of a neutral Austria is essential. This requires a foreign policy designed primarily to lay the foundations for the credibility and trustworthiness of Austria's neutrality both in peacetime and in possible crisis situations. The main elements of such a policy include strict adherence to neutrality and the duties arising from it, as well as a resolution to defend this neutrality with all possible means. This policy also means that relations with neighbouring states must be carefully cultivated and Austria must be established as a factor in international thinking by means of active participation in worldwide co-operation, especially within the framework of the United Nations. Finally, Austria's participation in pan-European co-operation represents an important element in her concept of a foreign policy.

The position that Austria has won for herself on the international scene since 1955 and the confidence that she now enjoys beyond her frontiers has shown that this concept was the right one. In recent years Austria has increasingly had a stabilizing function in Central Europe – the cockpit of the great ideological and power-political field of force of our day – and is increasingly becoming the venue for international meetings.

In order to achieve this most welcome result we had to gain the confidence of the governments of other states and also to stamp our new image on public opinion in the rest of the world. We achieved this by a consistent and comprehensive information policy designed to make people at home and abroad aware of the image of the new Austria.

These efforts naturally encountered the difficulty that Austria's great cultural inheritance and her long and glittering history were well known abroad, unlike the deep-seated changes that the country had undergone during the last fifty years in its political system, size and international status and its economic structure as a highly industrialized country. A new Austrian image must therefore be found to match up to her present-day international position.

As for the understanding shown by the Austrian public for her foreign policy since 1955 it must be remembered that – as we have seen – permanent neutrality represents a relatively new situation for the Austrian man-in-the-street: for centuries he had been used to seeing his country actively intervening in world politics. Yet in spite of the fact that the Austrian public is becoming increasingly aware of the country's international status, there does seem to be a need for promoting a deeper understanding of her policy of neutrality.

The difficulties we encountered in laying down a policy of neutrality and creating an image for Austria abroad are real enough even in periods of relative calm; they are doubly real in crisis situations, especially when these occur close to the borders of the neutral country.

For Austria, where no legislative or administrative measures have so far been decreed for such a crisis situation, the road of pragmatism would seem to hold the best prospects. In discussions of this subject in Austria the opinion has frequently been voiced that wild or unbridled criticism, unfounded sensational reports and personal insults merely serve to intensify existing tensions in the event of critical situations in foreign policy; thus they may exacerbate these tensions and complicate foreign policy – and in certain circumstances even jeopardize the country's independence. For a country such as Austria this is undoubtedly a very serious question and one that must be closely examined in each specific situation as it arises. I personally feel that the key to the problem lies in the establishment of a close relationship of trust between the government and the mass media.

In times of crisis in particular it is necessary to maintain continuous contacts between the two, whereby the maximum of information compatible with the secrecy required by national security should be made available to the mass media. Situations may arise, on the other hand, in which the information media should impose voluntary restrictions on themselves for the common good.

Successful co-operation of this kind naturally requires both personal contact and a clear and realistic foreign policy, which can be accepted as plausible and consistent by public opinion and in particular by the representatives of the mass media. It seems to me, therefore, to be one of the prime tasks of foreign policy to establish a fruitful relationship with the mass media, in order to place them in a position in which they can understand their country's foreign policy and judge it objectively. By doing so the mass media render a valuable service to their own people and also represent a vital factor in the shaping of foreign policy.

THE CONCEPT UNDERLYING AUSTRIA'S FOREIGN POLICY

I thought it right to discuss in some detail the special importance that public opinion has for a country's foreign policy. Any foreign policy can win through in the long run only if it enjoys the broad support of the people. The most brilliant and most appropriate foreign policy will prove worthless if it lacks public support because the public have not been adequately informed by the mass media. Naturally it is far more difficult for a neutral country like Austria to develop such a concept. I have already referred to the necessary process of readjustment that our people had to undergo in the foreign policy sphere following the collapse of the monarchy. As the subjects of a great and powerful empire we were directly or indirectly involved in virtually all European conflicts; after 1918 the Austrian people were suddenly faced with the fact that they belonged to a small and weak political entity which had better steer clear of all conflicts. Even then certain trends emerged that supported a neutral attitude to the great issues under dispute. But these trends did not develop beyond their initial stage because the Austrian people themselves did not believe that Austria was a viable entity and because nothing or very little was done by other countries, especially the great powers, to support the First Republic and give the Austrian people confidence in its viability. The First Republic therefore perished not because the Austrians did not support it but because they were simply not given a chance to develop their new state on a sound economic and political basis.

A totally new situation arose in 1945. It turned out that nations and governments do, after all, sometimes learn the lessons of history. For the first time the need for an independent Austria in the heart of Europe was realized – a country which would safeguard the balance of power. I have always held the view that Austria's independence was demanded not so much out of consideration for the country's inhabitants but rather from considerations of self-interest on the part of the great powers; because of her geopolitical situation in the centre of Europe, at the great intersections of East and West, Austria was quite simply indispensable to the maintenance of the political balance of power. None of the great powers would allow her to be abandoned to the sphere of influence of another country. Herein lies her destiny, but also the great challenge to her foreign policy. Austria's interests coincide with those of the great powers which signed the Austrian treaty in 1955. They wanted a sovereign independent Austria as much as she did. That was why – unlike the situation after the First World War – they provided the economic prerequisites that enabled her to create the Second Republic from the ruins of the Second World War by means of a great deal of hard work. The 1955 treaty and the declaration of neutrality were merely the logical outcome of an awareness that had been gaining ground among Austrians ever since the collapse of the monarchy – an awareness that our country's independence is indispensable not only to Austria herself but to the peaceful development of our sorely tried continent.

Austria's concept of foreign policy is therefore obvious. It involves strictly observing the 1955 treaty and following a credible policy of neutrality; it also rests on the interest that the great powers and her neighbours have in maintaining an independent sovereign Austria. A consistent foreign policy must continually endeavour to keep this interest alive, in the knowledge that the slightest mistake may result in incalculable consequences. To find the right way, to know the limits of her foreign policy and at the same time to avoid imposing on her people any kind of ideological constraint resulting from her international status – this is the great and responsible task of Austria's foreign policy. Up to now, thanks to the co-operation of the Austrian people with its political leaders, this task has been successfully carried out and the country has been brought to a state of prosperity such as it has never known throughout its history. After years of isolation from world events, Austria once more enjoys the highest respect in the international community and is one of the most stable countries in the world, both in home and in foreign affairs.

The task of Austria's foreign policy will therefore be to continue steadfastly along the road determined by this concept of foreign policy and in this way to make a valuable contribution not only to her own security but also to the peaceful development of the world.

14

A NEUTRAL LOOKS AT THE WORLD

The days when a country could afford to live in 'splendid isolation' and to shut itself off from world events are long past. As a result of headlong technological development the world has shrunk and crises and conflicts, wherever they occur, usually have a marked effect even on regions far away from the actual source of the crisis. In view of Austria's geographical situation at the intersection of the two great power blocs no Austrian can remain indifferent to international developments. After all, the fate of his country depends on what is happening in the world around him.

THE WORLD AFTER 1945

It is therefore obvious that ever since Austria regained her independence her foreign policy has supported any attempt to reach an international *détente*, in the conviction that in the long run she can develop fruitfully only in a relaxed international climate. Since the end of the Second World War world politics have undergone a great many changes. The wartime comradeship-in-arms of the Allies disappeared shortly after 1945. Differing interpretations of arrangements and agreements made during or at the end of the war led to friction and eventually to deep mistrust between the western powers and the Soviet Union. Once again the world witnessed the interesting phenomenon, by no means new to history, of allies falling apart after victory and making new alliances with the defeated powers. The western Allies founded Nato and admitted West Germany to this organization, while the eastern countries signed the Warsaw

Treaty, which embraced Hungary, Bulgaria and Rumania, i.e. countries which during the war had sided with Germany. In Asia an alliance was made between the United States and Japan. Ideological conflicts – and, even more, power-political ones – resulted in the cold war, which for many years paralysed all attempts to achieve *détente* or *rapprochement* leading to peaceful coexistence between East and West.

This negative trend in international relations also had its effect on the European economic situation. United States economic aid to Europe, which found its final visible expression in the Marshall Plan, was not accepted by Moscow. The East European states followed that example and did not participate. Instead they founded a separate economic organization, the Council for Mutual Economic Aid, or Comecon. This accentuated the gulf between Western and Eastern Europe, and it was further widened by the setting up of the European Economic Community in 1957. The emergence of the EEC also resulted in a loose association of the European countries that were outside the eastern bloc but were not able or willing to participate at once, or to participate fully, in European integration; this led to the founding of the European Free Trade Area. Instead of the abolition of customs barriers, which would have been in line with a sound economic policy, regional economic and customs areas were created on both sides, with the result that countries outside the regional groupings found themselves in a difficult situation. The influence of political decisions on economic development was once more revealed. The greater the tensions the more difficult it became to reach a *rapprochement* between the different economic blocs.

It was one of the more hopeful aspects of the sixties that the wrongheadedness of this policy gradually came to be realized in both East and West and that attempts began to be made, tentatively at first but with increasing persistence, to adopt a policy of *détente*. This did not mean that security aspects were disregarded on either side; indeed it was obvious that a *détente* was possible only if both sides were ready to defend themselves. The Khrushchev–Eisenhower era clearly revealed an intention to turn away from the cold war and find a road back to at least a minimum of co-operation. The Austrian treaty, signed in 1955, was the first visible sign of this policy and it helped to support the credibility of Soviet foreign policy in this direction. Austria seized her moment and made her contribution to this development – one more proof that even a small country may, by adopting a skilful foreign policy, make a positive step in the field of international relations. The Soviet withdrawal from the Finnish naval base of Porkkala was another step in that direction.

But co-operation between Moscow and Washington was short-lived. The notorious U-2 incident, the Cuban crisis and other matters resulted in a renewed hardening of relations between the two super-powers. Mutual accusations and a wave of mistrust prevented any further *rapprochement* for the moment. The Hungarian crisis had already brought about a worsening of the situation. Yet it is to the credit of the leading statesmen that despite many a misjudgement on one matter or another, the worldwide clash that the world appeared to be on the brink of facing at that moment was avoided.

At that time the United Nations was still, up to a point, playing the role that had been assigned to it when it was set up – to keep the peace and to work actively for peace. The armistice in Korea and the settlement of the crisis in the Congo point in that direction in spite of the criticism and negative aspects that attach to these operations. The great powers were still ready to take conflicts and international crises to the United Nations and to seek a solution with its aid, whether or not they were themselves directly involved.

Matters then evolved differently. Not only the great powers but other countries too became less and less prepared to let the United Nations discuss their problems or to solve international crises within the framework of the world organization. There is an increasing tendency, especially on the part of the greatest powers, to try to settle disputes and conflicts outside the United Nations. There was and is an increasing polarization between the super-powers. This is not to say that France and Britain have ceased to play a part; indeed both these great powers still have a most important role to play, frequently a mediating one, which should not be underrated. France, in particular, under General de Gaulle, was an important mediator or catalyst between East and West, and by her independent and often somewhat headstrong policy introduced new elements into East–West relations. Even though de Gaulle's aim to establish Europe as a third force in the international interplay of forces has not been realized, the independent line pursued by France has done much to reduce the polarization of world politics between Moscow and Washington. This policy – the policy of adopting a stand *between* the blocs – has repeatedly enabled France to play the part of mediator, as for instance in the Vietnam conflict, when Paris was chosen as the venue for the negotiations on Vietnam. Even though France's efforts have frequently failed to achieve their objectives, it must be stated that they have certainly been worthwhile in one way or another.

Britain, too, though she has lost much of her former influence, still has a role to play – a role which is her due after her centuries-old experience with nations in the most varied parts of the world and one which could certainly be of very considerable value to those concerned. In the solution of delicate colonial problems in particular London has shown wisdom and farsightedness. The transformation of her empire into the Commonwealth, in spite of all the difficulties involved, has borne fruit. Britain's reputation will undoubtedly depend on the skill and resolution she is prepared to bring to the solution of outstanding issues in Africa and Asia. These problems are now emerging with increasing clarity, especially in the United Nations, where the general line-up is increasingly shifting from an East–West confrontation to a North–South polarization, i.e. between the prosperous industrialized countries and the developing countries.

It is gratifying to note that attempts at decolonization have made marked progress, especially over the past two decades. The United Nations has been fundamentally transformed by the admission of a whole series of new African and Asian states. There is probably no other spot on the globe where the new picture of our world can be seen more clearly than in the United Nations. The new countries have become valuable members of the world organization in an astonishingly short time – though there is no denying the fact that their expectations are often disappointed. Here, I believe, lies the real problem of relations between the industrialized and developing countries. The dynamism of the latter is frequently not prepared to accept delays and is apt to result in majority decisions that cannot ultimately be put into effect – because of the reservations expressed by the very countries who would be in a position to implement them. As a result some resolutions made by the world organization have about them something of an abstract note: this leads to a situation in which resolutions are passed but fail to achieve the results their supporters hoped for. To achieve a greater readiness to make concessions on both sides must be the objective of future efforts by the world organization. The destiny of the United Nations will ultimately depend on a satisfactory solution of the problem of relations between the industrialized countries and the far more numerous developing countries. It will also depend very much on whether the United Nations can be made truly representative, truly 'universal'.

15

THE RECENT YEARS

Several important events have taken place on the world scene over the past two years.

The People's Republic of China, the most populous country on earth, emerged from isolation and took its place in the United Nations and its specialized agencies. During the same period the world witnessed with relief the development of direct contacts and visits between heads of state. As in the case of all human relations, this is a main avenue to better understanding, co-operation and ultimately friendship.

Between the United States and the USSR *détente* took several forms, among which the first ceilings set by the Salt Talks may prove to be an important landmark in limiting the arms race.

The United Kingdom and two other European countries decided to join the Common Market. Through this expansion, the Common Market will become one of the greatest economic and technological groups in the world, reflecting a greater stability in the political relations among its member states.

The ratification of the German treaties with the USSR and Poland removed a major stumbling block in East–West relations. This will contribute decisively to the setting up of the planned conference on European security and ultimately to the admission of the two German states to the United Nations. The old continent of Europe, torn and divided by war for so many centuries, is setting an example of stability and has become a dynamic force in the development of peaceful relations between diverse political and social systems.

Last but not least, with the representation of the People's

Republic of China and the prospect of the admission of West and East Germany, the United Nations, already almost universal, is on the way to becoming the greatest meeting-point of aspirations, preoccupations and co-operation in our multipolar, multi-cultural and multi-ideological world.

These are positive and reassuring signs and may well indicate that the stage is set for a new chapter in world history, the outlines and directions of which are still difficult to detect. Most important of all is the fact that we can take it as axiomatic that the big powers do not want war. This was proved true again during 1971 and 1972, when two very dangerous crises – Bangladesh and the escalation in Vietnam – did not spill over into wider conflagrations and did not interrupt the process of *détente*.

This does not mean that the world is out of danger. There are some promising and some very menacing elements in this transition period. It is true that the present *détente* is a great relief after the terrifying period of brinkmanship of the cold war. But highly explosive situations remain in several places and these must be ironed out and solved once and for all if this development is to be strengthened and accelerated. The Vietnam conflict is of concern to the entire world community and must be given top priority on the agenda of world affairs. Direct negotiations which for so long have failed to stop the bloodshed seem, at the time of writing, to have reached a stage where peace may be near. The moral pressure of the entire community of nations which was brought to bear on this conflict might have played a significant role in this development. However, many of the conflicts brought before the United Nations are still unsolved and have been so for much too long. The fact that they are in a stage of armistice or cease-fire is no real consolation. The unsettled question of the Middle East is a potential source of grave danger as well as an obstacle to the peaceful development of that region. The Suez Canal, a main world artery, has now been closed for five years. It is the duty of the parties concerned, with the help of the United Nations, to bring about a final settlement of this conflict on the basis of Security Council Resolution 242 (1967), and thus contribute to the process of world *détente* from which everyone will benefit. The settlement of the Cyprus issue is also long overdue.

But even if the existing conflicts were solved instantly and in a satisfactory way, the world would by no means be out of danger. There remain around the globe several areas of confrontation and conflict. In southern Africa apartheid and colonialism are of grave concern to the world community and are a retarding element in the role that Africa could play as a united continent in the world of today. The first meeting ever held by the Security Council away from its headquarters took place in Africa in 1972, with the aim of underlining this fact. Some countries in the world still have not achieved political stability and the peaceful acceptance of national boundaries, a development that it took some older countries centuries and several wars to achieve. As a matter of fact some of the gravest international crises in recent years have been due to these factors. Such crises do not take place in a vacuum. Each of them prompts 'positions' from other nations and also from world public opinion, which has become a new major element in world affairs.

It is therefore the duty of the international community to act with restraint, to understand these growing pains, to help by healing the deeper causes, which are often poverty and despair, and to use the United Nations fully to diagnose, forestall and solve such troubles. A prevented conflict, even if it does not show on the credit side of international efforts, is a thousand times preferable to an actual conflict. But the patient must be brought to the clinic in time, not when it is too late.

Thus, in the short term we find both reassuring and disturbing elements. The neutral and smaller countries, which depend for survival and security on world peace and co-operation, must necessarily do and favour anything that contributes to the healing of existing wounds and to the improvement of international relations and friendship. Hopefully, by gaining time the much-needed historical adjustment in the world-wide play of power will take place and future world wars will be avoided. Despite the lack of tranquillity in our era, we must not forget that a world war has now been avoided for twenty-seven years in the most populous, most complex and most rapidly changing human society our globe has ever seen. Has this been due to the balance of terror, or is the human race at long last beginning to learn to live in peace on its planet? Whatever the cause or combination of causes, the fact is that the idea of a world war has receded dramatically from the minds of the leaders of our time.

THE LONG-TERM PROSPECTS

Nothing would be more dangerous than to underestimate the adverse currents that still disturb international relations. The arms race has not yet come to a halt. It is merely that its rate of increase has diminished, and ceilings have been set for certain weapons. While several highly industrialized countries have proved that they can live perfectly well without atomic arms, others believe that the possession of such arms is the only way to protect themselves effectively and to allow themselves to play an important role in the world. The treaty on the non-proliferation of nuclear weapons has been adopted by many countries, but some of them have stopped short of ratification, for they see military atomic power as a safeguard for their independence. A multipolar world is becoming visible in which 'greatness' can be measured in various ways: by atomic power, satellite technology, gross national product, scientific and industrial development, population, size of the market, resources endowment and so on. The world of power is in flux. What may be a weakness today, for example in the realm of population, may be a strength tomorrow if multiplied by industrial achievement. What may be greatness today, such as high industrialization and high personal income, may be a weakness tomorrow if the human environment and man's dignity are impaired. Many combinations of powers, large and small, political, economic and others are conceivable and will probably be attempted at one time or another in our complex world. At present, for example, some of the small and medium powers are afraid that a *rapprochement* between the big powers may be detrimental to them. Conversely, the increase in the number of small and medium powers in the United Nations and the consequent change in the predictable voting balance is considered one of the reasons for the diminishing support of the organization by the big powers.

No one can predict in which direction these forces, crisscrossed as they are by ideological and cultural trends as well as by new power and wealth groupings such as multinational corporations, will develop. For the first time in history even the concept of 'winner' and 'loser' may perhaps begin to lose much of its meaning. However difficult the task, it is up to the political

leaders to guide these forces into peaceful and constructive channels and to take the people's aspirations for peace, justice and
progress one step further. This task, precisely because it is world-
wide and of unprecedented difficulty, is one of the most thrilling
challenges that have ever confronted politicians. We must become
used to living in an extremely complex world subject to constant
change, innovation and correction, in which national government
and responsibilities are deeply interwoven with the affairs of
the planet as a whole.

In this rapid evolution we can discern several trends that will
bind humanity closer together while at the same time creating
unprecedently serious problems for governments.

Above all our era is determined by the phenomenal pace of
scientific and technological progress and by the continued spread
of the industrial revolution to the furthest areas of the globe. Over
the past twenty-five years more technological progress has been
made than during the entire previous history of mankind. Elec-
tronics, antibiotics, space technology, computers, the harnessing
of atomic energy and supersonic transport are all inventions of
the last twenty-five years.

These and a hundred other developments have changed human
life and its prospects on a scale and at a speed never experienced
before. The benefits for man have been immense. Despite deep
disparities between North and South, his average life expectancy
has dramatically increased. The world death-rate has greatly
diminished. The amount of goods and services provided for the
individual in the industrialized societies is staggering.

One beneficial result for humanity as a whole has been the
world-wide spread and interdependence of knowledge, events and
aspirations. Peoples and nations know each other better today
than they have ever done before. Revolutions in communications,
transport and tourism have brought people closer together and
have reduced the barriers of ignorance and prejudice. It is universally recognized today that people in the poorer countries
have the same rights as others to higher standards of living, a
problem that barely preoccupied the developed countries before
the Second World War. Mankind has witnessed the blossoming
of a host of solidarity movements between countries: aid to
developing countries, aid for children and refugees, aid in the case
of natural disasters, reconstruction after conflicts. A close inter-

dependence of events has taken place all over the globe: a war, a conflict, a natural disaster, persistent violation of human rights can no longer take place in isolation. Public opinion and governments are more and more concerned with such events. A strong desire for peace, respect, reciprocal understanding and justice pervades the world. It is less and less easy to convince the younger generation, the first global generation, that there are issues which justify the killing or oppression of other young men.

More and more people are becoming aware of the fact that the world has become a closely knit interdependent unit in which each person, each group, each nation and each continent is dependent on another. This is a new, very fundamental reality brought about by science and technology. It has no parallel in any earlier period of history. It is bound to change our political thinking, attitudes, relations and institutions profoundly. For many centuries isolated and independent ways of life could prevail in most regions of the world, without impinging on each other. This period has gone for ever. Today the world is crisscrossed by streams of news and communications by means of image and sound, prodigious movements of goods, men, fashions, ideas, inventions and more recently waves of public opinion and moods. This trend is irrevocable and irreversible. The dream of isolation or immunity from world events is gone for ever. The sovereignty of nations is overflown daily by thousands of aeroplanes and satellites. World interdependence is growing day after day through visible and invisible links between peoples all over the world. It still remains, however, for political thinking and behaviour to adapt fully to this new reality.

Another consequence has been that we have entered into an unprecedented era of mass phenomena. This era began with the industrial revolution, when after millions of years of evolution man started to proliferate after having discovered the means of transforming the earth's physical and living conditions on a large scale for his own benefit. We are familiar with the population explosion or with the fact that 140 years ago humanity had reached only 1000 million people; that it took the next hundred years to reach the second 1000 million, thirty years to reach the third 1000 million; that by the year 1975 we shall be 4000 million and by the end of this century in all probability 7000 million people.

H

The consequences of this phenomenon are staggering and they are accompanied by a series of other revolutions or explosions, such as the urban explosion and transport explosion and the consumer explosion. The statistics published by the United Nations and its specialized agencies show that most world totals in these fields have at least doubled or tripled over the last twenty years. World agricultural production has doubled, world industrial production has tripled, world exports have quadrupled, petroleum output has quintupled. Projections for the future indicate further upward changes in practically every direction. Humanity seems to have stepped into a new era in the history of our planet, the era of mass phenomena due to the multiplication of the human race.

This has recently given rise to a new problem of world-wide concern: that of the environment. True enough, this problem was primarily created by the highly industrialized countries, which consume two-thirds of the world's resources and whose citizens are responsible for between twenty and fifty times more pollution of the natural elements than those of the poorer parts of the world. But standards of living are rising everywhere. The industrial revolution continues to spread. The population figures of the developing countries may some day be multiplied by high consumption figures. United Nations statistics and experts tell us, for example, that the annual increase in world population requires an additional consumption of water equal to that carried by a medium-sized river. We also learn that every day 20 pounds of riverborne pollution reach the oceans for every man, woman and child in the United States and Canada; in a week this represents the approximate equivalent of the weight of an average person. We can easily visualize the result for a world of 7000 million people that has reached a standard of living equal to that of North America today, unless there is a change in present production processes and consumption habits!

The time is therefore past when a nation could assume that its individual actions would have no effect on the community of nations. The oceans, the seas, the atmosphere, our rivers and our earth, whose resources we thought were unlimited and could be tampered with impunity, suddenly appear as a joint property, as a common heritage of mankind. From space the astronauts brought back the first global pictures of our earth, which simply showed a few continents surrounded by 70 per cent water and by a fragile atmosphere. They revealed no borders. Humanity is suddenly discovering that its actions and powers are not unlimited on this planet; that our life-sustaining elements and resources are finite; that many delicate balances bind the physical and biological phenomena of our earth. We had thought for a very long time that human control over the elements was the ultimate practical aim. We saw our world as a very large place to live in, with unlimited possibilities. The discovery of atomic energy seemed to confirm us in this belief. But now scientists and biologists have a different evaluation. They show us a very thin layer of life-bearing elements, the biosphere, which reaches only 300 feet deep into the oceans, and 9000 feet into the atmosphere. In that layer 95 per cent of all life on earth and perhaps of our solar system is concentrated. We also learn that some of the relationships and cycles that bind the atmosphere to the oceans, the earth to the atmosphere and our lives to the elements may henceforth run the risk of being irremediably damaged by our massive interventions. A world concern for the planet has thus arisen in recent years which begins to overshadow in many minds conventional thinking with regard to power, influence and wealth. Is it not one of the great ironies of all time that in such circumstances mankind should not be able to solve conflicts such as Vietnam and the Middle East and spend 200,000 million dollars each year on armaments? Future generations will be right to ask, when looking back to our era: 'Were they blind?'

It is therefore difficult to believe that governments, especially those of the big powers, will not soon face the real problems and begin to co-operate honestly and actively under the pressure of these growing concerns. National priorities can no longer be isolated from world priorities. Governments must sit together, examine these new problems and work together lest these common menaces overtake and defeat their national objectives, plans and concerns. The present process of *détente* is hopefully a first sign of that wisdom.

It should come as no surprise that in the wake of the scientific and industrial revolution views and ideologies should have arisen that claim to know how world society should be conceived and organized in order to achieve peace, progress and social justice.

One view claims that freedom and private enterprise alone will do the job; others say that all decisions must come from the top in order to ensure that all people have equal access to resources; yet others believe that the solution lies somewhere in between. Each of these systems may still harbour the hope for the collapse of the others. It is a matter of urgency to set aside this fallacy and to accept instead the pragmatic truth that mankind is likely to be immensely damaged by our common problems before any of the present armed camps collapses. The arms race and military nuclear power have created not only a balance of terror but a balance of ideologies. For each of them it is too late to hope for world expansion and for the defeat of the others. To continue to cling to this illusion is to achieve the contrary of what is desired, as we can see today: conflict, distrust, wasteful armaments, uncured poverty in the South of the globe, subversion, violence and a lack of proper world-wide co-operation and action. Rather than claiming to possess exclusive access to the truth, would it not be better to confess that we are all in the same boat, confronted with the most gigantic and complex problems humanity has ever seen and to which there may be many answers in our multi-cultural world?

Nobody can pretend to possess the whole truth. Man and society have always been and will always be changing and dissatisfied. On the eve of our concerns becoming world-wide there can be no more urgent requirement for statesmen than peace. The time has therefore come for governments and the representatives of the different social and political systems to sit down together, to exchange their experiences honestly, to enrich each other in the difficult art of governing men in a global, proliferating society and to support our co-operative and collective instruments, the United Nations, its various agencies and the regional organizations.

Peaceful coexistence is no longer sufficient. It is peaceful co-operation among all systems and governments that is needed. Some may say that this would give the edge to those who in recent years have asserted their power through armaments, especially nuclear power. This is not true, for the tendency to greater unity and community on our planet is accompanied by a deep-seated concern to preserve the individuality of people, cultures and nations. One of the greatest characteristics of our time is the emancipation and enrichment of the individual through education and freedom from want; another is the strong desire of groups, cultures, nations and languages to withstand the melting-pot tendencies of scientific and technological change and to save from the past whatever does not stand in the way of progress. A world is thus taking shape in which there will be both greater unity and greater diversity, more concern with the future and with the past, more welfare and more preoccupation with the preservation of nature, culture and the arts. Science has shown that it is possible to advance dramatically both into the infinitely large and into the infinitely small. Political and human relations cannot lag behind. The world is taking on a form in which nations, big or small, northern or southern, eastern or western, are settling down into a peaceful pattern of cultural diversity in which we should see not an obstacle to the unity of men but an enrichment of our society. Peace, justice and progress on our planet do not require uniformity and the crushing of values inherited from the past. On the contrary, in the reorientation of our priorities considerably more resources will have to be devoted to preserving that diversity. The concept of the natural environment of man should be expanded into a concept of cultural environment which includes the treasures and achievements of the arts and of the past. All these preoccupations are found in the United Nations and in its agencies, which are designed to protect the national and cultural diversity of our planet while fostering peace, understanding and justice.

It is generally acknowledged that international peace, justice, order and development in the world are prerequisites for the survival and welfare of small countries. It has been Austria's experience that working actively towards these aims while remaining outside big power groups not only strengthens the independence and prosperity of a country but also contributes to a relaxation of tensions and a general improvement in the international climate. It might be an example that can point the way to new approaches to the goal we are all striving to reach: international peace, justice and prosperity.

Notes

1

BIRTH FROM CHAOS

1   For the portrayal of events in 1918 and subsequent years I have used among other books Erich Zöllner, *Geschichte Österreichs. Von den Anfängen bis zur Gegenwart* (Vienna 1970); Hans Leo Mikoletzky, *Österreichische Zeitgeschichte. Vom Ende der Monarchie bis zur Gegenwart* (Vienna 1969); Walter Goldinger, *Geschichte der Republik Österreich* (Vienna 1962).

2   See 'Wie alt ist Österreichs Neutralität?' Rechtsgutachten Nr. 39, Sozialwissenschaftliche Arbeitsgemeinschaft (Vienna, n.d.), pp. 18ff.

3   See Edvard Beneš, *Der Aufstand der Nationen* (Berlin 1928).

4   See *Bericht über die Tätigkeit der Deutschösterreichischen Friedensdelegation in St Germain en Laye*, 2 vols. (Vienna 1919).

5   On the *Anschluss* problem see Friedrich F. G. Kleinwächter and Hans Paller, *Die Anschlussfrage in ihrer kulturellen, politischen und wirtschaftlichen Bedeutung* (Vienna 1930).

2

AUSTRIA'S STRUGGLE FOR EXISTENCE

1   For the defence associations see Heinrich Benedikt, *Geschichte der Republik Österreich* (Vienna 1954), pp. 359ff.

2   See also Viktor Miltschinsky, *Das Verbrechen von Ödenburg* (Vienna 1922).

3   For the period 1933-8 see also Hans Huebmer, *Österreich 1933-1938. Der Abwehrkampf eines Volkes* (Vienna 1949); Ulrich Eichstädt, *Von Dollfuss zu Hitler. Geschichte des Anschlusses Österreichs 1933-1938* (Wiesbaden 1955); Kurt Schuschnigg,

Im Kampf gegen Hitler: Die Überwindung der Anschlussidee (Vienna, Munich, Zurich 1969).

4 See also Julius Deutsch, *Der Bürgerkrieg in Österreich* (Karlsbad 1934).

5 Heinrich Siegler, *Österreichs Weg zur Souveränität, Neutralität und Prosperität 1949-1959* (Bonn, Zurich, Vienna 1967), p. 10.

3
A COUNTRY IS WIPED OFF THE MAP

1 See Mikoletzky, *Österreische Zeitgeschichte*, p. 382.

2 See Gerald Reitlinger, *The Final Solution: The attempt to exterminate the Jews of Europe, 1939-45* (London 1953).

3 See Otto Molden, *Der Ruf des Gewissens. Der Österreichische Freiheitskampf 1938-1945* (Vienna, Munich 1958).

4
THE END OF THE WAR: A NEW START

1 See 'Wie alt ist Österreichs Neutralität?' p. 30.

2 Gerald Stourzh, 'Zur Entstehungsgeschichte des Staatsvertrages und der Neutralität Österreichs 1945 bis 1955', *Österreichische Zeitschrift für Aussenpolitik*, 5/6, (1965), pp. 276ff.

3 Stourzh, in *Österreichische Zeitschrift*.

4 Stourzh, in *Österreichische Zeitschrift*.

5
THE STRUGGLE FOR A TREATY

1 Stourzh, in *Österreichische Zeitschrift*, pp. 303ff.

2 Siegler, *Österreichs Weg.*, p. 10.

3 Stourzh, in *Österreichische Zeitschrift*, p. 306.

4 Siegler, *Österreichs Weg*, p. 13.

5 Stourzh, in *Österreichische Zeitschrift*, p. 306.

6 Siegler, *Österreichs Weg*, p. 16.

7 Siegler, *Österreichs Weg*, p. 16.

8 Bruno Kreisky, 'Österreichs Stellung als neutraler Staat' in *Österreich in Geschichte und Literatur*, 3 (1957).

9 Wolfgang Strasser, *Österreich und die Vereinten Nationen* (Vienna 1967), p. 7.

10 Strasser, *Österreich*, pp. 9ff.

11 Siegler, *Österreichs Weg*, p. 19.

12 Bruno Kreisky, *Die Herausforderung* (Düsseldorf 1963), p. 96.

13 Kreisky, *Herausforderung*, pp. 93ff.
14 Kreisky, in *Österreich in Geschichte*.
15 Walter Goldinger, *Geschichte der Republik Österreich* (Vienna 1962), p. 279.
16 Stourzh, in *Österreichische Zeitschrift*, pp. 282ff.
17 Stourzh, in *Österreichische Zeitschrift*, pp. 327ff.
18 *Keesing's Contemporary Archives* (1955), pp. 5,006ff.
19 Kreisky, in *Herausforderung*, p. 101.
20 Federal government statement in the *Wiener Zeitung* for 16 March 1955, quoted in *Keesing*, p. 5,073.
21 *Keesing*, p. 5,073.
22 Sven Allard, *Diplomat in Wien* (Cologne 1965), p. 173.
23 Allard, *Diplomat*, p. 175.
24 Allard, *Diplomat*, pp. 145ff. (especially p. 157); see also Stourzh, in *Österreichische Zeitschrift*, p. 328.
25 Siegler, *Österreichs Weg*, p. 22.
26 Siegler, *Österreichs Weg*, p. 22.
27 Stourzh, in *Österreichische Zeitschrift*, pp. 331ff.
28 Alfred Verdross, *Die immerwährende Neutralität der Republik Österreich* (Vienna 1966), p. 9.
29 Verdross, *Neutralität*, p. 9.
30 Siegler, *Österreichs Weg*, p. 283.
31 Stourzh, in *Österreichische Zeitschrift*, pp. 322ff.
32 Siegler, *Österreichs Weg*, p. 283.
33 Siegler, *Österreichs Weg*, pp. 26ff.
34 Stourzh, in *Österreichische Zeitschrift*, pp. 322ff.
35 Siegler, *Österreichs Weg*, p. 24.
36 Allard, *Diplomat*, pp. 238ff.
37 Kreisky, *Herausforderung*, p. 102.
38 Kreisky, *Herausforderung*, p. 103.
39 Alfred Maleta, *Entscheidung für morgen*, (Vienna, Munich, Zurich 1968), p. 167.
40 Maleta, *Entscheidung*, p. 159.
41 Maleta, *Entscheidung*, p. 185.
42 Kreisky, *Herausforderung*, pp. 105ff.

6

AUSTRIA AND PERMANENT NEUTRALITY

1 Verdross, *Neutralität*, p. 3.
2 Verdross, *Neutralität*, p. 5.

3 From the shorthand record of the sessions of the National Assembly, VIIth legislative period (1955/IV), p. 9.

4 Appendix no. 520 to the shorthand record of the sessions of the National Assembly, VIIth legislative period.

5 *Federal Law Gazette*, 211 (1955).

6 Verdross, *Neutralität*, p. 9.

7 Verdross, *Neutralität*, p. 10.

8 Verdross, *Neutralität*, pp. 13ff.

9 Verdross, *Neutralität*, pp. 15ff.

10 Erik Castrén, 'Neutralität', *Archiv des Völkerrechts*, 5 (1955–6); Karl Zemanek, 'Wirtschaftliche Neutralität', *Juristische Blätter*, 81 (1959), p. 250.

11 Lujo Tončić-Sorinj, 'Neutralität zwischen Ost und West', lecture to the Foreign Policy Society in Bonn (28 February 1967); Verdross, *Neutralität*, p. 17; Zemanek, in *Juristiche Blätter*, 81, p. 250.

12 Documents of the San Francisco Conference, VI, pp. 418, 459 and 722.

13 Verdross, *Neutralität*, p. 25.

14 Tončić-Sorinj, 'Neutralität'; Verdross, *Neutralität*, p. 27; Josef L. Kunz, 'Austria's Permanent Neutrality' in *American Journal of International Law*, 50 (1956), pp. 418–25.

15 Tončić-Sorinj, 'Neutralität'.

16 Verdross, *Neutralität*, pp. 30ff.

17 Verdross, *Neutralität*, pp. 30ff.

18 Max Nef, *Verschiedene Gestalten der Neutralität* (1956), p. 20.

19 Verdross, *Neutralität*, p. 32.

20 Kreisky, 'Die Österreichische Neutralität', lecture to the Economic Society of Zurich (4 May 1960).

21 Siegler, *Österreichs Weg*, p. 36.

7

FOREIGN POLICY *VIS-À-VIS* THE FOUR GREAT POWERS

1 On the significance of Austria's geographical position see Hugo Hassinger, *Österreichs Wesen und Schicksal, verwurzelt in seiner geographischen Lage* (Vienna 1949); Hans Bobek, *Schlüsselstellung in Europa, Lage und Raum* (Vienna 1957).

8

AUSTRIA AND EUROPEAN INTEGRATION

1 *Wiener Zeitung* (1 August 1961), p. 1.

2 *10 Jahre österreichischer Integrationspolitik, 1956–1966*, a collection of documents relating to the federal ministry of trade and reconstruction, pp. 105ff.

3 *10 Jahre*, pp 110ff.

4 *EEC Bulletin*, 1 (1962), p. 39.

5 *10 Jahre*, pp. 127ff.

6 *Wiener Zeitung* (4 April 1963), p. 2.

7 *Wiener Zeitung* (23 April 1963), p. 2.

8 *10 Jahre*, pp. 244ff.

9 Summary of the result by E. P. Hochleithner, *Österreichische Zeitschrift für Aussenpolitik*, 4/5 (7th year), pp. 273ff.

10 On 10 May 1967; strictly speaking the first application for admission since the application of 10 August 1961 merely dealt with the opening of negotiations to examine the possibilities for admission.

11 Item 14 of the Hague Communiqué, *EEC Bulletin*, 1 (1970), p. 16.

12 *Wiener Zeitung* (4 December 1969), p. 3.

9
THE SOUTH TYROL

1 On the South Tyrol problem see Franz Huter (ed), *Südtirol—Eine Frage des europäischen Gewissens* (a collection of essays by Ermacora, Huter, Stadlmayer, Veiter and others) (Vienna 1967); Karl-Heinz Ritschel, *Diplomatie um Südtirol* (Stuttgart 1966); Renato Cajoli, *Die Autonomie des Trentino-Tiroler Etschlandes* (Bologna 1952); Mario Toscano, *Storia diplomatica della questione dell' Alto Adige* (Bari 1967); Siegler, *Österreichs Weg;* Strasser, *Österreich.*

2 Siegler, *Österreichs Weg.*

3 The 'international court agreement' stipulates that the international court's jurisdiction for international disputes, arising from the European convention on the settlement of disputes, also extends to disputes arising from agreements—such as the Paris agreement—concluded before the convention came into force.

12
ECONOMIC AID TO THE DEVELOPING COUNTRIES

1 Lester B. Pearson (Chairman), *Pattern in Development*, Report of the Commission of International Development (New York 1969).

2   'Report on the Sixth Session' of the Committee for Development Planning, 49th Session, Economic and Social Council, Supplement No. 7, United Nations (New York 1970).

3   Rudolph A. Peterson (Chairman), 'US Foreign Assistance in the 1970s: A New Approach', report to the president of the United States from the Task Force on International Development (Washington D.C. 4 March 1970).

4   Sir Robert Jackson, *A Study of the Capacity of the United Nations Development System*, United Nations Document DP/5 vols. I and II, (Geneva 1969).

5   Pearson, *Pattern in Development*, p. 27.

6   Pearson, *Pattern in Development*, pp. 31 and 49.

7   Pearson, *Pattern in Development*, p. 48.

8   *Federal Law Gazette*, 342 (1969).

9   *Federal Law Gazette*, 251 (1966).

10 Werner Melis, *Österreichs Wirtschaftsbeziehungen mit den Entwicklungsländern* (Vienna 1970), p. 21.

11 Melis, *Österreichs Wirtschaftsbeziehungen*, p. 24.

12 Pearson, *Pattern in Development*, p. 38.

13 Pearson, *Pattern in Development*, p. 41.

14 *Österreichische Forschungsstiftung für Entwicklungshilfe*, 5/6/7 (1970), pp. 48 and 71.

15 Melis, *Österreichs Wirtschaftsbeziehungen*, p. 67.

16 Melis, *Österreichs Wirtschaftsbeziehungen*, p. 73.

MAPS

The Habsburg Empire

The successor states

Europe in World War II

'Greater German Reich' 1939

Allies of Germany

Occupied territories

U.S.S.R. before 1939

Acquisitions since 1939

250

miles

Europe after 1945

N O R

DENM

North Sea

Hambur

BRITAIN

Amsterdam

London

NETHERLANDS

FEDER

Brussels

REPUBLIC

BELGIUM

OF

Oise

GERM

Paris

Rhine

Loire

Elbe

F R A N C E

Berne

SWITZERLAND

Rhône

Milan

S P A I N

NATO States

Warsaw Treaty States

250

miles

INDEX